A Guide to
BEIJING

COLLINS

8 Grafton Street, London W1

William Collins Sons & Co. Ltd
London · Glasgow · Sydney · Auckland
Toronto · Johannesburg

British Library Cataloguing in Publication Data

A Guide to Beijing. — (China Guides Series)
1. Beijing (China) — Description —
Guide-books
I. Series
915.1'1560458   DS795.A4

ISBN 0-00-217945-8

Series Editors: May Holdsworth and Jill Hunt

Text by David Bonavia, Judy Bonavia, Caroline Courtauld, Shann Davies, Seth Faison Jr,
May Holdsworth, Simon Holledge, Jill Hunt and Diana Martin

Cover photograph by Paul Lau

Photographs by Magnus Bartlett (6, 21, 24−25, 32, 37, 45, 51, 58, 63, 74−75, 95, 100, 109,
112, 126); Anthony Cassidy (5, 7, 54 top three, 82−83, 114, 123); The Commercial Press,
Ltd (8−9, 71, 89, 90, 133); Ingrid Morejohn (13, 16, 70); Jacky Yip (10, 28, 29, 44, 48, 54,
66, 78)

Design by Joan Law Design & Photography

Printed in Hong Kong

Contents

Traditional snacks remain a favourite with Beijing children

Roofs of the Imperial Palace

*One of the figures lining the
Spirit Way at the Ming Tombs*

Names and Addresses

In this book addresses are given in
Pinyin. Dajie is a main thoroughfare;
lu is a road and *jie* is a street; *hutong*
and *xiang* are lanes and alleys.

Names of hotels and restaurants
are also given in Chinese characters
in the text to help visitors getting
about on their own. Names of all the
sights, shops and other places
described in the book are given in
Chinese characters in the Index of
Places.

大江

Life in Beijing

David Bonavia

Beijing is a city in the process of converting itself from a dignified, venerable metropolis into a bustling modern capital city — one of the most populous in the world. From the thronging crowds in the shopping areas around the city centre, to the massive rows of new housing projects, there is a sense of purpose where previously the emphasis was on the picturesque.

Not that modern Beijing is not picturesque — some of its ancient buildings and parks are among the loveliest anywhere on earth. But in the 1980s the accent is on bringing about better living conditions for the roughly 10 million population. And in this context tourists are welcomed in ever increasing numbers to help supply the huge financial resources required for modernization.

Despite the growing demand for bright and colourful clothing, and modern household equipment like refrigerators and washing machines, Beijing retains an air of dignity which it acquired over the past seven centuries. And as the heart of a nation of more than a billion people, it self-consciously strives to be the finest and most modern city in China.

But leave the main boulevards and plunge into the network of residential *hutongs* (alleys), and you will find a series of interlocking villages, where families cluster in old-fashioned compounds behind their thick, grey-plastered walls, sometimes with carved stone lions flanking the red gateways.

The best way to catch Beijing unawares is to slip out at dawn and go for a walk in the alleyways. One will come upon a single person or a whole group doing *taiji* or Chinese shadow boxing callisthenics. They will ignore you as you walk by unless you lift a camera, in which case they will instantly stop their exercise.

The camera-shyness of the Chinese varies from place to place and from time to time. Foreigners used to be mobbed in most places outside Beijing by inquisitive local citizens. This has in general been stopped, and many Chinese do not like the idea of having their picture printed in some foreign magazine. They prefer anonymity, and in Beijing they nowadays barely give the foreigner a fleeting glance.

Another good reason to get up early is to watch the city's workers eating breakfast at fast-food stalls — mostly just a steamed bun, an elongated doughnut, or a bowl of rice-gruel with a little pickle for flavouring. From the houses of those who take breakfast at home comes the heavy odour of coal-dust, as a thin trickle of smoke seeps from the outlet-pipes under the eaves.

In the outskirts, new blocks of brick and concrete apartments stand up squarely against the sky. The flats are tiny by most standards, but nearly everybody wants one, for to live in the big city is considered a great stroke of luck or a privilege. A subway runs from the main railway station to the biggest steel-works, in the western outskirts. Jeeps, official cars, and trolley-buses — but most especially bicycles — jostle for their place on the street. Where once a thin line of traffic dawdled along huge, half-empty thoroughfares, there are nowadays traffic jams which curt, energetic policemen attempt to sort out.

Under the present leadership, prosperity and consumerism are the order of the day, if only on a modest level. Luxury consumer goods have been imported, and not just for sale to foreigners with hard currency. Privately-owned motor scooters have made their appearance. Where once it was hard to find a cab, there are now thousands of them plying for hire.

The modern face of Beijing may seem less interesting to visitors who have come to view the magnificent historical relics. But for the majority of the inhabitants, it is the more prosaic aspects of society that govern their lives, while the palaces and parks of long-gone emperors are simply places of recreation for the family at weekends.

The river of bicycles, which takes over the streets in the rush hours, ebbs somewhat as the commuters give way to crowds of shoppers. Some may be buying a piece of pork or fish and spring onions for their midday meal, though the majority of workers eat at their place of employment and take a nap before resuming work. Great attention is attracted by the display windows of a Japanese watch company, at the studios of wedding photographers, and of course at the clothing stores.

For some years past Chinese women have been eschewing the drab trouser-suits in blue or grey, which were supposed to strengthen the feeling of anonymity and uniformity. Now this policy has been reversed and young people in particular are encouraged to wear attractive and colourful clothes, if only to raise their sense of optimism and zest in living. However, the more outlandish modern western fashions are frowned upon, though China has already entered the world fashion market with model-shows and visits by famous foreign couturiers.

At weekends, the busy city relaxes a little, as families pour out to the lakes and gardens of Beihai Park, or the Summer Palace, or just take their children strolling among the flowerbeds and bare earthen knolls of some lesser amenity. The more ambitious catch a bus all the way out to the Great Wall — a half-day trip — or to the ethereally lovely Ming Tombs, taking photographs of each other in stiff, formal poses and, of course, eating and drinking. A snack, be it a loaf of bread, an ice-cream or slices of watermelon in the summer, is an essential feature of any outing, and most excursions quite naturally end up as picnics.

In the winter some people still bundle up and go skating on the frozen lakes; this helps warm them because most Chinese homes are chilly through lack of coal. Warmth is supplied sparingly from iron stoves filled with anthracite, which are also used to keep kettles simmering gently all day. A cup of hot water — with a few tea leaves as a luxury — is regarded as a fine way to refresh oneself and settle the digestion. The Chinese rarely drink cold water, and this helps keep infectious diseases away.

In the summer, though, the men roll up their trouser legs while the women and girls flap themselves with their loose skirts — and sit dreamily on the doorstep in the evening, catching a breath of air before settling down for the night.

The pleasantest times of the year are spring — when the shrubs suddenly burst into tiny blossoms and the big, mechanized water-carts turn out to keep down the dust and nourish the newly-planted saplings along the streets — and early autumn, when the humid heat of the Beijing summer gives way to a gentle wind from the Fragrant Hills to the west and the trees turn mellow red and orange before losing their leaves. As the weather gets colder, the persimmon orchards twinkle with bright, golden fruit whose sweet pulp is a great favourite with local people.

Partially replacing the big red propaganda billboards of a decade ago, advertising now enlivens the grey and ochre shades of the buildings. Hopeful western and Japanese business firms believe that advertisements may bring their product to the attention of some official empowered to import from abroad, and familiarize the public with their brand names.

Numerous small private restaurants have sprung up in recent years, and old Beijing hands say they are better and much cheaper than the famous old eateries with their specialities of close on a dozen different Chinese provinces — including, of course, the famous Beijing duck. Even Maxim's of Paris has opened a branch in Beijing, though few local people could afford to eat there — it is used mainly by foreign businessmen.

In the eastern part of the city there are now several big, modern luxury hotels with discos and western cuisine. Alas, for many foreigners in Beijing they have become the centre of social life, and fewer people nowadays bother with the fine old Chinese restaurants. But wherever you eat, drink, go shopping or sightseeing, Beijing has preserved enough of its past to make a visit there unforgettable.

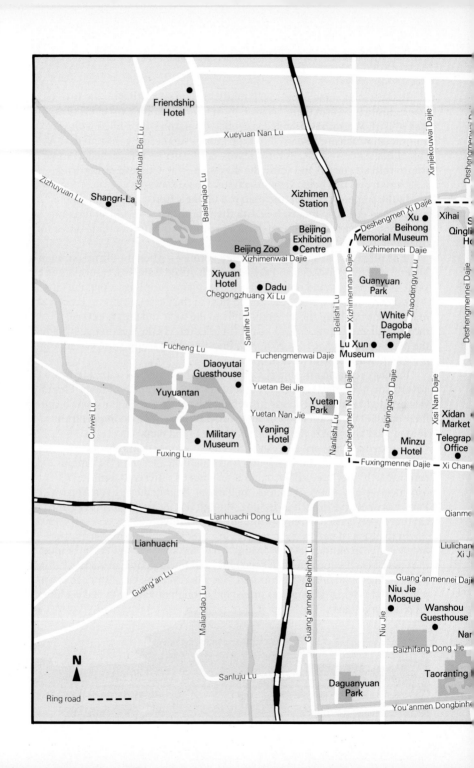

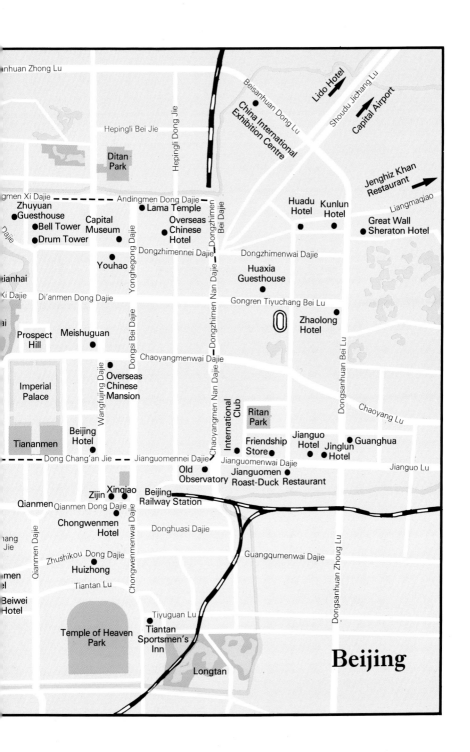

Getting to Beijing

By air The number of direct flights to Beijing has increased dramatically in the past few years. A full list of airlines serving Beijing is given in Useful Addresses on pages 137—138.

China's own carrier, CAAC (the Civil Aviation Administration of China) now has 27 international air routes. Despite efforts to improve, including the purchase of many new modern aircraft, the airline's erratic service often falls short of accepted standards, particularly on domestic flights. CAAC's ground handling can be both irritating and inefficient, but is hard to avoid since the airline still has sole ticketing and booking rights within China for many of the foreign airlines flying to Beijing. CAAC takes a tough line with no-shows — if you miss your flight, the ticket is void and cannot be transferred to another flight.

CAAC's main office is at 117 Dongsi Xi Dajie (tel. 553275, open 8 am—5:30 pm daily). Staff here are notorious for surly service, and even the simplest of transactions may take several hours. CAAC also has offices in the Beijing Hotel, west building (tel. 5007317, open 9:30—11:30 am, 1—6 pm, closed Sundays). CITS and a few of the other agencies listed in Useful Addresses on pages 138—139 will purchase CAAC tickets for you (for an additional fee).

The most popular air route to Beijing is from Hong Kong on Cathay Pacific or CAAC. Flying time is under 3 hours. When direct flights are full, there is an alternative route via Tianjin (on CAAC) which adds one hour to the journey. Another possibility is to fly via Guangzhou (Canton) or Shanghai but obviously this takes longer.

A new Beijing-based civilian airline, United China Airlines, set up by the airforce, has domestic flights to a number of cities including Hangzhou, Wuxi and Shenzhen.

Taxis are readily available at Beijing's Capital Airport and the fare to the city centre is around Rmb40. A few hotels have an airport shuttle bus, and others will send a car if prearranged.

By rail Beijing can also be reached by train from Hong Kong, via Guangzhou. Through tickets may be booked in Hong Kong (around US$100 first-class), and the journey takes 36 hours from Guangzhou. From Hong Kong to Guangzhou takes around three hours. A first-, or 'soft', class sleeper on Chinese trains offers you an old-fashioned, but comfortable, berth in a four-berth compartment, and reasonable Chinese food in the restaurant car. If time is not a factor, this is an interesting way to see China's richly varied countryside. Beijing-bound trains leave Guangzhou at 6 pm and 9 pm every evening.

Once in Beijing, taxis are available at the railway station. The taxi stand is to the right of the station exit.

Return rail tickets from Beijing cannot be bought outside China, but it is not difficult to make the purchase in the capital. There is a special foreigners' ticket office at the rear of the main station central hall, where the staff speak good English. Or, for a small additional fee, you may ask a local travel agent, such as CITS, to buy it for you. Trains fill up fast, so tickets should be booked several days in advance.

Foreigners are also permitted to travel to Beijing by train from Pyongyang, from Ulan Bator on the trans-Mongolian railway, and from Moscow on the trans-Siberian railway. But long-distance travel by road is not yet allowed for foreigners in China.

General Information for Travellers to Beijing

Visas

Everyone must get a visa to go to China, but this is usually an easy, trouble-free process. Tourists travelling in a group are listed on a single group visa — a special document listing all members of the group — which is issued in advance to tour organizers. Individual passports of people travelling on a group visa will not be stamped unless specifically requested.

Tourist visas for individual travellers (those who are not travelling in a group) can be obtained directly through Chinese embassies and consulates, although some embassies are more enthusiastic about issuing them than others. Certain travel agents and tour operators around the world can arrange individual visas for their clients. It is simplest in Hong Kong, where there are a large number of travel agents handling visa applications. Just one passport photograph and a completed application form are necessary. The need for exit visas for foreigners leaving China was dropped in 1986.

Visa fees vary considerably, depending on the source of the visa, and on the time taken to get it. In Hong Kong, for instance, some travel agents can get you a tourist visa in a few hours, but it may cost around US$30, while a visa which takes 48 hours to obtain might cost just US$9.

The visa gives you automatic entry to all China's open cities and areas (there were 436 in 1987). Travel permits to certain areas of China, which used to be needed in addition to the visa, were dropped in 1986.

The mechanics of getting a business visa are much more flexible than in the past, particularly in Hong Kong. The applicant should have either an invitation from the appropriate Foreign Trade Corporation (several now have permanent representatives abroad), or from the organizers of a specialized trade fair or seminar. In Hong Kong, all that is needed is a letter from the applicant's company confirming that he wishes to travel to China on business.

Regular business visitors are eligible for a multiple re-entry visa which may be obtained with the help of a business contact in China. Some Hong Kong travel agents can also arrange re-entry visas for clients — the cost might be around US$50—60.

A business visa is also issued on arrival in Beijing, as long as the businessman brings with him a supporting invitation with the application. However, Chinese immigration officials have described this service as a fall-back for businessmen who do not have time to get a visa in advance, and they do not expect large numbers of tourists to use it.

Single-entry tourist visas are generally for a period of 30 days, but can be extended once you are in China. Single-entry business visas are normally valid for three months, while multiple re-entry visas may be for three or six months.

Customs

A customs declaration form must be filled out by each visitor upon entry — the carbon copy of this form will be returned to you and it must be produced at customs for inspection on departure from China.

Some personal possessions that you are asked to list on arrival — such as tape recorders, cameras, watches and jewellery — must be taken out with you when you leave. When you arrive you will be told at immigration which items these are, and they may be inspected by customs officials on departure from China.

Four bottles of alcohol, three cartons of cigarettes, unlimited film and unlimited medicines for personal use may be taken in. Firearms and danger-ous drugs are strictly forbidden. It is also illegal to acquire Chinese money abroad and take it in, or to take any out of the country.

Money

Chinese Currency The Chinese currency, which is sometimes referred to as Renminbi or Rmb, meaning 'people's currency', is denominated in *yuan* which are each divided into 10 *jiao*, colloquially called *mao*. *Jiao* are, in turn, each divided into 10 *fen*. There are large notes for 10, 5, 2, and 1 *yuan*, small notes for 5, 2, and 1 *jiao*, and coins for 5, 2 and 1 *fen*.

Currency Certificates Foreign Exchange Certificates (FEC) were intro-duced in 1980. These were designed to be used instead of Renminbi by foreigners, Overseas Chinese and Chinese from Hong Kong and Macao only, for payments in hotels, Friendship Stores, at trade fairs, and for airline tickets, international phone calls, parcel post etc. In practice, however, FEC quickly became a sought-after form of payment anywhere, and a black market developed between Rmb and FEC. In September 1986 it was an-

nounced that FECs were to be phased out, but shortly afterwards a post-
ponement was announced, so the fate of FEC remained unclear.

FEC and Rmb may be reconverted into foreign currency or taken out
when you leave China, but it is impossible to change them abroad.

Foreign Currency There is no limit to the amount of foreign currency you
can bring into China. It is advisable to keep your exchange vouchers as the
bank may demand to see them when you convert Chinese currency back into
foreign currency on leaving China.

All the major freely negotiable currencies can be exchanged at the
branches of the Bank of China, in hotels and stores.

Cheques and Credit Cards All the usual American, European and
Japanese travellers cheques are acceptable. Credit cards are accepted in a
limited number of Friendship Stores, hotels and banks. You should check
with your credit card company or bank before you rely on this form of payment for your purchases. Personal cheques are sometimes taken in return
for goods which are shipped after the cheque is cleared.

Tipping Tipping is forbidden in China.

Communications

Telecommunications

Beijing's local telephone system has not kept pace with the general rapid
development in the city. There are simply too few lines so making a local call
can be a time-consuming and frustrating experience. An additional com-
plication has resulted from the current telecommunication expansion programme which has involved changing many of Beijing's telephone numbers.
Your hotel may be able to help you find up-to-date numbers. Or you could
try dialling information on 114 (local calls), or 116 (long distance). The
China Phonebook, published in Hong Kong, and available in some hotels in
China, is the best source for business telephone numbers in the city.

International calls from Beijing are not as difficult as domestic calls. The
staff on the international exchange are usually helpful, and most speak good
English. Rates are high, but it is possible to transfer charges. A handful of
major hotels now have International Direct Dialling (IDD) to Japan and
Hong Kong. But phoning to Beijing from outside China tends to be a very
long process.

Most hotels will place long-distance and international calls for you. This
usually involves filling out a form which you then give to the floor staff. You
then wait in your room for the call to be put through.

The wave of new hotels opening in the city has brought a welcome in-
crease in telex installations, although some hotels are only equipped for
outgoing transmissions. Not all hotels have a telex operator prepared to send

telexes for guests, so you may have to punch your own telex tape. A few hotels have fax machines (see Hotels pages 26–38).

There is a 24-hour telecommunication office at Xidan, for telephone calls, cables and telexes. Other Post and Telecommunications offices are given in Useful Addresses on page 140.

English-language Media
The English-language Chinese newspaper, *China Daily*, began publication in mid-1981 and is available at all hotel magazine kiosks. *Newsweek*, *Time* and a number of international magazines, newspapers and paperback novels are also on sale at hotels or at the Foreign Languages Bookstore at 219 Wangfujing, very near to the Beijing Hotel. The Chinese themselves publish magazines about China in English as well as books on a wide variety of subjects, some political, some not.

Travel Agencies

There are a number of State-owned corporations which handle foreign visitors to China, but the largest is China International Travel Service (CITS) — also known as Luxingshe — which until recent policy changes had the monopoly on handling foreign tourists. Other large organizations which handle foreign visitors are China Travel Service and China Youth Travel Service. Addresses of these, and other agencies, are given in Useful Addresses on pages 138–139.

CITS offers a comprehensive service covering accommodation, transport, food, sightseeing, and special visits to schools, hospitals, factories, and other places foreigners might be interested to see. They also provide services such as ticket sales for walk-in customers.

Most foreign tour operators work with CITS to arrange group itineraries; CITS do all the ground handling once in China. With the pressures of rapidly developing tourism, it is hard to finalize all the arrangements in advance, and tour groups may find alterations are made to the flights or the hotel that has been programmed.

The Beijing Tourist Bureau has set up two complaints desks, tel. 5122211 ext. 260 (hotels), 336009 (restaurants).

Climate and Clothing

Beijing has four clearly defined seasons. From November to March, winter is usually dry and clear but winds from the northwest can bring temperatures down to −15.5°C (−4°F). The best winter clothing is layers of warm garments including thermal underwear, sweaters and coats, in addition to warm boots and fur hats with earflaps. Heating in the hotels can be very fierce. The

Chinese produce good winter clothing such as thick cotton underwear, padded jackets and furs, all at reasonable prices.

Spring usually lasts from mid March to mid May and is a good time for a visit, with trees and flowers coming into bloom and the occasional shower to wash the city. Clothing should include a warm coat and sweaters as well as some light-weight clothes, and possibly a raincoat.

Beijing summers are very hot and humid. Temperatures reach 40°C (104°F) and rainfall is light. Light, cotton clothing is recommended. Visitors will often be in places without air-conditioning.

Autumn is the best season in the capital. From September to mid October it is warm, sunny and dry. There is a wealth of colour in the parks, and fruit and flowers in the markets. Dress as you would for autumn in southern Europe or northern California.

Beijing has a large diplomatic community as well as many business visitors, so to that extent it is more formal than other Chinese cities. The Chinese do not mind whether visitors dress formally or informally, as long as they are neat and do not show too much flesh.

Average Temperatures in Beijing

		C°	F°		C°	F°		C°	F°
Average	JAN	−4.4	24.1	MAY	18.9	66.0	SEP	19.1	66.4
High		1.7	35.1		25.3	77.5		25.5	77.9
Low		−9.7	14.5		11.9	53.4		12.2	53.8
Average	FEB	−2.1	28.2	JUN	23.9	74.5	OCT	12.2	53.9
High		3.8	38.8		29.6	85.3		18.7	65.7
Low		−7.2	19.0		17.7	63.9		6.8	44.2
Average	MAR	4.7	40.5	JUL	25.6	78.1	NOV	4.3	39.7
High		1̵1.0	51.8		30.3	86.5		10.0	50.0
Low		−0.9	30.4		21.5	70.7		−0.2	31.6
Average	APR	13.0	55.4	AUG	24.0	75.2	DEC	−2.5	27.5
High		19.4	66.9		28.9	84.0		3.0	37.4
Low		6.5	43.7		19.9	67.8		−7.0	19.4

Hotels

Over the past few years there has been a rapid surge of hotel construction in
Beijing in an attempt to keep pace with demand from the fast-increasing
number of visitors who flock to the capital. Beijing's hotels offer the visitor
quite a choice of quality and price, ranging from the upmarket Shangri-la or
Sheraton, down to utilitarian hostelries where you may stay, dormitory-style,
for a few *yuan*. Quality of management covers an equally broad spectrum. In
some hotels you will find polite, well-intentioned (possibly well-trained)
English-speaking staff; in others, management still pays little attention to
cleanliness, maintenance, or charm.

Beijing Municipality says there are 64 hotels in the city which accept
overseas guests, but in practice some of these are not keen to have foreigners
stay there, while others could only be recommended as a last resort when
everywhere else in the city is full.

Beijing's top hotels are mostly financed from overseas and run by foreign
management groups. With overseas staff (many are from Hong Kong) in top
managerial positions, these joint-venture hotels are aiming at international
standard service and facilities — and they charge international prices for
them.

The new joint-venture hotels have the great advantage of a workable
confirmed booking system — always a major difficulty for non-group
travellers in China. As a rule, it is difficult to get confirmed bookings for
Beijing's Chinese-run hotels, even though more travel agencies, including
CITS, can now arrange bookings for a select few. Attempts by individuals to
get bookings confirmed by letter or telex still tend to go unanswered.

In peak months (March through to November), rooms in the capital have
been very hard to come by. Although the shortage should ease as more hotels
open up over the next few years, it is still advisable for travellers who want a
good hotel to book it as far in advance as possible.

Some of Beijing's older hotels, run by the municipality, have been ins-
pired by standards set by new hotels, and have made visible efforts to improve — though none seem entirely able to throw off the quirks of hotel
management Chinese-style.

Chinese-run hotels typically have private bathroom, telephone, heating,
and sometimes air-conditioning. Boiled drinking water is placed in each
room. There are outlets for electric razors, the current being 220 volts.
There are TV sets in the public lounges and sometimes in rooms. Room
service is patchy, but one can usually get beer and soft drinks until late at
night by approaching the floor-attendants who look after most services.
There are small shops, bank, postal and telegraph facilities in the hotel
foyers. To make a long-distance call, you complete a form at the floor-
attendant's desk and then wait in your room. Chinese and western food is

available, and private dinner parties and banquets can be arranged. Standard meal charges will be in the range of Rmb50 per day, exclusive of drinks and special dishes. (Plain food is relatively cheap in China.) A range of imported foreign wines and spirits, Coca-Cola, cigarettes and films can be bought at special stalls in most big hotels and Friendship Stores. Some hotels also stock overseas newspapers and magazines.

In many Chinese hotels, the attendants have an irritating habit of opening the door one has carefully locked. Try not to be annoyed — they are confident that no-one is going to interfere with your possessions. But be prepared for attendants walking into your room with barely a knock, and even dusting around while you are trying to change.

The following list of hotels gives an approximate range of rates for rooms and suites in late 1986, to be used as a basis for comparison, rather than an accurate picture of current prices. Only special facilities (beyond TV, bank, post office, hairdresser, tourist shops) have been mentioned.

Superior

Great Wall Sheraton
Donghuan Bei Lu,
Chaoyang
tel. 5005566,
tx. 20045,
fax 5001938, 5003398

长城饭店
朝阳东环北路

1007 rooms, US$100–850, executive floor, business centre, nightclub, Clark Hatch health centre, indoor/outdoor swimming pool, tennis, billiards, theatre (max 900), ballroom (max 1800), conference and banquet (max 1000). (Amex, Diners, Visa, Mastercharge, Federal, Great Wall Card)

With a vast reflective glass facade, impressive pyramid-shaped atrium lobby, scenic elevator, and plush interiors, this is one of Beijing's smartest hotels. Opened at the end of 1983, Sheraton took over management in mid 1985. Its many facilities include restaurants offering French, Sichuan, Cantonese, and international cuisine, together with a 24-hour coffee shop. Location is good for business visitors and tourists alike — a few minutes' taxi-ride from the fast developing Jianguomenwai business area, and from the new exhibition centre in the north-eastern suburbs, and 10–15 minutes' drive to Tiananmen.

Shangri-la
29 Zizhuyuan Lu
tel. 8021122,
tx. 222231,
fax. 8021471

香格里拉饭店
紫竹院路29号

Jianguo
Jianguomenwai Dajie
tel. 5002233,
tx. 22439

建国饭店
建国门外大街

786 rooms, US$80−380, business centre, health club and indoor swimming pool, music room, ballroom and function rooms (max 750). (Amex, Visa, Mastercharge)

The newest of Beijing's joint-venture hotels, this fully opened in 1987 under the management of the Shangri-la International Group, who run a number of Asia's top hotels. The attractively designed rooms in the main building are very spacious, and amongst the best in Beijing. The smaller west building has 76 guestrooms and 44 fully equipped office suites, which may be rented by the day or on long lease. The hotel is in the northwest part of the city, near the old exhibition centre, and Erligou Negotiations Building. It is 10−15 minutes by car to Tiananmen, and about 40 minutes to the airport. Restaurants include a brasserie, coffee shop, and the Shang Palace offering high-quality Chinese food (a hallmark of Shangri-la hotels).

457 rooms US$85−185, ballroom (max 200) indoor swimming pool, delicatessan. (Visa, Diners, Amex)

Opened in April 1982, this was the first foreign-managed hotel in Beijing, and is a favourite with business visitors and the few independent travellers who are lucky enough to get a room. Competition to secure a booking is fierce year-round. Despite the Jianguo's modest appearance, the Peninsula Group management has built up a reputation for quality food in the Cantonese, Japanese and European restaurants and in the coffee shop. Its bar — Charlie's — is one of the best in town. The Jianguo is within walking distance of Beijing's two major new office blocks for foreign companies — the CITIC Building and Noble Tower — and a few minutes' taxi-ride from Tiananmen. The distance from the airport is 25 kilometres (16 miles).

**Dragon Spring
Mövenpick-Radisson
Guesthouse**
Shuichi Bei Lu,
Mentougou
tel. 8773480

龙泉宾馆
门头沟水池北路

*235 room and suites, US$60−70, conference (max
500) and banqueting (max 160) facilities, indoor pool,
tennis courts, health club, billiard room, secretarial
services*

Beijing's first international-style hotel with a
Chinese architectural design, located near the
Fragrant Hills about an hour's drive from
Tiananmen, opened in early 1987.

**Jinglun
(Beijing-Toronto)**
Jianguomenwai Dajie
tel. 5002266,
tx. 210012, cable 5650

京伦饭店
建国门外大街

*695 rooms, US$90−190, business centre, ballroom
(max 400). (Visa, Mastercharge)*

Next door to the Jianguo, the joint-venture
Jinglun is smoothly run by the Japanese hotel
group, Nikko. Opened in 1984, it rapidly became
another business visitors' favourite, because of its
convenient location and quietly efficient service.
Book as far in advance as possible. Like the
Jianguo, the building itself is unremarkable, but
the food is amongst the best that Beijing's hotels
offer.

**Holiday Inn Lido
Beijing**
Jichang Lu, Jiangtai
Lu, tel. 5006688,
tx. 22618

丽都假日饭店
机场路将台路

*1000 rooms, US$77−175, health club, bowling
centre, indoor swimming pool, billiards, TV games,
supermarket, delicatessen, disco. (Amex, Diners, Visa,
Mastercharge)*

The Lido Hotel, opened in 1983, officially became a Holiday Inn in 1985 when the hotel had
reached a standard that satisfied the Holiday Inn
Group management. This very successful operation is the largest Holiday Inn in Asia. The whole
complex is a massive expatriate enclave, with
offices and residential apartments, a large sports
club, as well as hotel rooms. Located in an un-
developed area northeast of the city centre, the
hotel is 20−30 minutes' journey into town. The
new exhibition centre is nearby. A hotel shuttle
bus service takes guests to key stops downtown.
The Lido has a reputation for good food with a
smart European restaurant, a coffee shop, noodles
and congee restaurant, and a quality Cantonese
restaurant.

Beijing Hotel
Dongchang'an Dajie
tel. 507766, tx. 22426,
cable 6531

北京饭店
东长安大街

910 rooms, Rmb100−300. Business centre, conference and banqueting hall (max 1000)

First opened in 1917, this is undoubtedly the capital's grand old hotel. It is ideally located for the business visitor and tourist alike, at the corner of Beijing's main shopping street Wangfujing. A number of foreign companies have their representative offices here. Rooms are almost impossible to secure without a contact in the city — the hotel rarely confirms bookings from individuals outside China.

The giant complex has three wings, with a fourth under construction. The west wing was built in the early '50s, and the east wing (remarkable for its electronically controlled curtains and firy central heating) was opened in 1974. Recent renovations have smartened up the gloomy public areas, while the service (reputed to be surly at best) has noticeably improved, even extending to room service after midnight. The restaurants offer a whole range of Chinese regional dishes, as well as Japanese and European food.

Diaoyutai State Guesthouse
(Angler's State Guesthouse) Sanlihe Lu tel. 668541

钓鱼台国宾馆
三里河路

Rooms from US$100. Extensive gardens, lake (fishing and boating)

A few select tour groups and business delegations stay in this secluded guesthouse complex, until recently reserved for high-ranking Chinese officials and visiting guests of the Chinese government. Many VIPs are still housed here, and guests may be aware of special security measures. The buildings are set in attractive wooded parkland, which date back to the 11th century. Many of the public rooms and suites contain exceptionally fine Chinese antiques — furniture, paintings, bronzes and porcelain. Food is restricted to Chinese cuisine, and service is, of course, excellent. The rarefied atmosphere here would not appeal to anyone who wants to feel at the centre of the action, but for a taste of a refined, and privileged, Chinese life-style, there is nowhere to equal the Angler's State Guesthouse.

Club Méditerranée,
Nanhu Island,
Summer Palace,
Yiheyuan tel. 281931,
281936

南湖宾馆
颐和园

US$100 (double), 23 rooms and suites, restaurant and conference (max 30)

Club Med has achieved the apparently impossible, by taking on management of two small villas right in the Summer Palace grounds — Nanhu Villa is on the picturesque small island in the middle of Kunming Lake (connected to the mainland by an arched bridge), and Jiqingxian Villa is near the east gate, close by the Garden of Harmonious Interest. Both villas — which are completely self-contained — have been restored without losing the Chinese flavour of the original. Several Club Med managers were brought in to head up the local staff and train the cooks. The villas, which together accommodate 36 guests, are open to any business visitor or tourist.

First-Class

Kunlun Majesty
21 Liangmaqiao,
Chaoyang
tel. 5003388,
tx. 210327

昆仑饭店
朝阳亮马桥21号

1005 rooms, US$110-200, health club, swimming pool (indoor), tennis courts, nightclub, ballroom and conference facilities (max 120)

Fully opened in March 1987, this large Chinese-owned hotel is almost a mirror image of the Great Wall Sheraton, which is on the opposite side of the road. The Kunlun's rates and range of facilities rank it with Beijing's top hotels. A number of foreign managers have been brought in to run what will be a massive operation, but first signs are that management will not match the Sheraton's polish.

Zhaolong
2 Gongren Tiyuchang
Bei Lu, Chaoyang
tel. 5003976,
tx. 210219

兆龙饭店
朝阳工人体育场北路

270 rooms, Rmb230-650, theatre (max 200), banquet (max 300), health club, indoor/outdoor pool

This modern new hotel, a gift from Hong Kong shipping magnate Y.K. Pao, had an auspicious start when Deng Xiaoping attended its opening at the end of 1985. Well located near the Jianguomenwai business area, the rooms and public areas are attractive, and the young Chinese manage-

ment enthusiastic. It has European, Japanese and Chinese food.

Fragrant Hills (Xiangshan) Hotel
Xiangshan tel. 819242, tx. 285491, cable 7391

香山饭店
香山

288 rooms, Rmb130−240, health club, outdoor pool, tennis, gardens

I.M. Pei's masterpiece blend of Chinese and western architecture is set in the former hunting park at the Fragrant Hills, some 20 kilometres (12 miles) northwest of Beijing. This is a long way out for anyone who wants to travel to the city centre everyday (usually at least an hour by taxi), but the magnificent setting has its compensations. Since it opened in 1982, service and maintenance have not been adequate for this unique lowrise building which is visibly beginning to suffer from neglect, but the Chinese management now promises improvement.

Xiyuan
Erligou tel. 868821, tx. 22835, cable 8766

西苑饭店
二里沟

750 rooms, Rmb165−1650, health club, indoor swimming pool, business centre

Another Great Wall Sheraton look-alike (except that this top-floor restaurant section actually revolves), this glass-fronted tower opened in 1984. Much of the construction work and interior designs were done with foreign assistance, but the hotel is entirely run by local management. Service and maintenance, sadly, are no match for the quality of the building. The older section of the hotel has 500 recently renovated rooms. The location is ideal for business visitors who need to be near the Erligou Negotiations Building or the old exhibition centre and is some 5 kilometres (3 miles) from Tiananmen.

Standard

Zhuyuan Guesthouse
24 Xiaoshiqiao Hutong, Jiugulou Dajie
tel. 444661, cable 3428

竹园宾馆
旧鼓楼大街小石桥胡同24号

39 rooms, Rmb80−350

In a pictuesque part of the city (near the old Bell and Drum Towers), this was the former residence of the disgraced Chinese leader, Kang Sheng. Its Chinese-style covered walkways and gardens are charming and, weather permitting, food can be served outside on a garden terrace. Bookings through CITS are sometimes accepted, but usually it requires *guanxi* (connections) to get in here.

Huadu
8 Xinyuan Nan Lu
tel. 5001166,
tx. 22028, cable 5431

华都饭店
新源南路 8 号

522 rooms, Rmb80−170, ballroom and conference (max 500), banquet (max 50)

Built and run by CITS, this hotel caters predominantly to CITS tour groups. Opened in 1982, the Huadu was the first hotel in this developing diplomatic quarter in the northeast. (The Great Wall Sheraton and Kunlun are nearby). Facilities have suffered from heavy use.

Friendship Hotel
Baishiqiao Lu
tel. 890621, cable 2222

友谊宾馆
白石桥路

1500 rooms, Rmb66−145, outdoor swimming pool, gymnasium, theatre, tennis

This massive Russian-style complex in extensive grounds dates back to 1952. It accommodates tourists, business visitors and some resident foreign teachers. This is a relaxed, pleasant place to stay, specially in summer, with a good range of facilities. Its distance from the city centre is the main drawback, although the hotel's newly introduced shuttle bus service has partially eased transport difficulties.

Minzu
51 Fuxingmennei
Dajie tel. 658541,
tx. 20091/2,
cable 8541

民族饭店
复兴门内大街51号

615 rooms, Rmb86−350, conference and banquet (max 400), gym, billiards

Lengthy renovation and extension works on this older hotel were completed in 1985. But the new interiors have not affected the Minzu's reputation for casual service, or for palatable reasonably-priced food (specially in the European restaurant). The hotel is centrally located — five minutes or less by taxi to Tiananmen — and guests are predominantly long-staying businessmen.

Qianmen
1 Yongan Lu
tel. 338731

前门饭店
永安路１号

460 rooms, Rmb120−280

This was partially under renovation in 1986, although still accepting guests. Work is due to be completed in 1987. It is well located, just 1 kilometre (less than a mile) from the Front Gate, and near Liulichang (Beijing's best-known antiques street). To date, neither facilities nor service have been specially noteworthy.

Xinqiao
2 Dongjiaomin Xiang,
Chongwenmen
tel. 557731

新桥饭店
崇文门东交民巷２号

320 rooms, Rmb113−337, conference and banquet (max 300), health centre, boulangerie

Located in the old Legation Quarter, this hotel was opened in 1954. Renovation work was underway in 1986, but the hotel was still accepting guests. The new Japanese restaurant and café (which serves Japanese noodles and snacks) is already open, and the Lion Bar now serves Japanese beer. Because Pakistan International Airlines crews used to be put up here, the western restaurant runs to curries and chappattis.

Zijin Binguan
(formerly Guesthouse
no 14) 9 Chong-
wenmen Xi Dajie
tel. 549215

紫金宾馆
崇文门西大街９号

17 rooms, Rmb260−350 full board

Centrally located, this guesthouse mostly has long-staying business guests.

Yanjing
2 Fuxingmenwai Dajie
tel. 868721, tx. 2100,
cable 5046

燕京宾馆
复兴门外大街 2 号

Yanxiang
2 Jiangtai Lu
tel. 5006666,
tx. 210014, cable 1500

燕翔饭店
将台路 2 号

Youhao Binguan
7 Houyuanensi,
Jiaodaokou tel. 441036

友好宾馆
交道口后园恩寺 7 号

507 rooms, Rmb150−280

Opened in 1981, this austere building (originally planned as an office block) is quite centrally located about 5 kilometres (3 miles) west from Tiananmen. It is primarily used by long-staying businessmen and Japanese tour groups.

515 rooms, Rmb150−280, ballroom (150), banquet (max 300), indoor swimming pool

This pleasant prefabricated hotel, opened in 1981, continues to expand, mainly as a tourist hotel for less expensive tour groups. Although rather far out, it is next door to the Holiday Inn Lido, where there is a downtown shuttle bus, as well as plenty of taxis.

50 rooms, Rmb100−180

This charming guesthouse was the residence of Chiang Kai-shek when he visited Beijing. It has a secluded location, set in a courtyard down a small *hutong* in the north of the city. The Japanese restaurant in the adjoining Baiyun Guesthouse is particularly good. All guesthouse reservations are handled by the Chinese People's Association for Friendship with Foreign Countries.

Budget Hotels

Beiwei
Beiwei Lu tel. 338631

北纬饭店
北纬路

226 rooms, Rmb93−210

This hotel is reasonably well located in the southern part of the city centre, near Liulichang, and the Temple of Heaven. It has Chinese and western food, and recent renovation work has improved its uninviting rooms to make it one of the better budget hotels in the city.

Dadu
21 Chegongzhuang
Dajie, Xicheng
tel. 890981

大都饭店
车公庄大街21号

433 rooms, Rmb70−210, ballroom (max 200), banquet (max 350)

Opened in 1984, this is an unpretentious place with pleasant service, in the west of the city, near the Xiyuan.

Guanghua
38 Donghuan Zhong
Lu tel. 592931

光华饭店
东环中路38号

204 rooms, Rmb45−110

Popular with budget travellers, this is a simple, clean and friendly hotel. The Chinese dining room serves a western breakfast.

Huilongguan
Deshengmenwai
tel. 275931

汇龙观
德胜门外

350 rooms, Rmb86−100

In the northern suburbs of Beijing, this modest new hotel is a long way out for tourists (15 kilometres or 9 miles from the city centre) but it is reasonably well run.

Huizhong Hotel
120 Zhushikou Xi
Dajie tel. 337131

惠中饭店
珠市口西大街120号

300 rooms, Rmb60−120

No western food served here, but facilities put this at the top end of the budget hotel range. It is a new hotel, just to the south of the city centre.

Nanhua
11 Nanhua Xi Lu,
Hufang Lu, Xuanwu
tel. 337916, 332619,
cable 7916

南华饭店
宣武区虎坊路南华西
路11号

50 rooms, Rmb120−180

Located in a small *hutong* near the Qianmen Hotel, this small, new hotel has friendly staff who welcome foreign guests.

Overseas Chinese Hotel (Huaqiao Binguan)
5 Santiao Beixinqiao

175 rooms, Rmb100−190

Despite its name, this modest hotel in the interesting Xinqiao area does accept bookings from foreigners.

tel. 446611

华侨宾馆

北新桥三条 5 号

Overseas Chinese Mansion (Huaqiao Dasha)
2 Wangfujing Dajie
tel. 558851

华侨大厦

王府井大街 2 号

190 rooms, Rmb13 (dormitory)−Rmb158

This only takes foreigners 'in emergencies' but is a convenient location for budget travellers.

Qiaoyuan
Youanmenwai,
Dongbinhe Lu

侨园饭店

右安门外东滨河路

200 rooms, Rmb8 (dormitory)−Rmb32

Another favourite with backpackers, even though the location is rather out of the way. It has a pleasant setting, and offers friendly service.

Tiantan Tiyu Binguan (Sportsmen's Inn)
10 Tiyuguan Lu
tel. 752831, tx.22238,
cable 3128

天坛体育宾馆

体育馆路10号

100 rooms, Rmb36−82

This guesthouse in a pleasant residential area was originally used to house visiting sports delegations, but now is a favourite with back-packers. Its Chinese restaurant serves a western breakfast.

Wanshou
12A Wanshou Lu
tel. 812901

万寿宾馆

万寿路12A号

80 rooms, Rmb70−170

A good hotel for a budget traveller, although a little out of the way.

Other possibilities are:

Ziyu 5 Huayuancun, Xisanhuan Bei Lu
tel. 890191, tx. 22078
125 rooms, Rmb50−110, opened in 1984
紫玉饭店　西三环北路花园村5号

Chongwenmen 2 Qianmen Dong Dajie
tel. 5122211
65 rooms, Rmb68−148
崇文门饭店　前门东大街2号

Capital Airport Hotel Shoudujichang
210 rooms, Rmb60−120 (under renovation)
首都机场饭店　首都机场

Beijing Exhibition Centre Hotel
135 Xizhimenwai Dajie tel. 890661
250 rooms (under renovation)
北京展览馆饭店　西直门外大街135号

Peace Guesthouse 3 Jinyu Hutong, Dongdan
Bei Dajie
(under renovation)
和平宾馆　东单北大街金鱼胡同

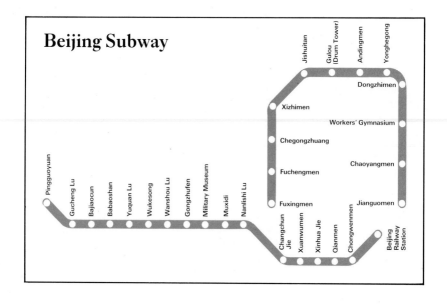

Beijing Subway

Getting Around

Most visitors use taxis to get around Beijing. Other forms of transport can turn out to be more of an adventure than a rapid means of getting to a particular destination on time.

The number of taxis in the city has increased dramatically in the past few years — according to municipal statistics, there are over 200 taxi companies in operation. Taxis range from Chinese-style curtained limousines to racy Peugeots, Toyotas or Mercedes. During the day there are usually plenty of taxis at the places frequented by foreigners — outside major hotels, sights, office buildings, restaurants. But if you stray off the normal tourist track, it is safer to ask the taxi to wait. The charge involved is small, but during the busy tourist season, the driver may refuse to do so. In this case, you could call the English-speaking central office of the Capital (Shoudu) Car Company — tel. 557461 — and they should send a taxi for you. Some taxis respond to being hailed in the street, while others do not.

Taxi rates have risen rapidly, doubling in little over a year. In 1986 it was 80 *fen* a kilometre (0.6 mile), increasing to Rmb1.20 after 10 kilometres (6 miles). Taxis may also be hired for a day, or half day. Your hotel should be able to arrange this. The cost was around Rmb100 a day in 1986.

Although Beijing's subway, which links the main railway station with the western and northern suburbs, serves only a small part of the city, it is worth a try if your journey happens to coincide with the stops. Stations are named in *Pinyin*, so are recognizable even if you do not read Chinese characters. There is a standard fare, and tickets are bought before getting on the train (see map on page 38).

Buses and trolleybuses are more difficult to handle for newcomers to the city, partly because of the dense, pushing, crowds that use them at most times of day and night, but also because fares are based on the distance you intend to travel. If you cannot speak Chinese, get someone to write down your destination to show to the ticket collector when you get on. The collector might also help you get off at the right spot. A map showing the capital's complex bus and trolleybus system is usually available in hotel bookstores.

A more adventurous way for energetic tourists to see the city is by bicycle. There are a number of bicycle hire shops used to catering to foreigners. One which is conveniently located is the Jianguomenwai Bicycle Repair Shop just across the street from the Friendship Store. It is open 7:30 am–6 pm and a bicycle costs Rmb2 a day. Another favourite with foreigners is Limin, at 2 Chongwenmenwai Dajie, not far from the Xinqiao Hotel.

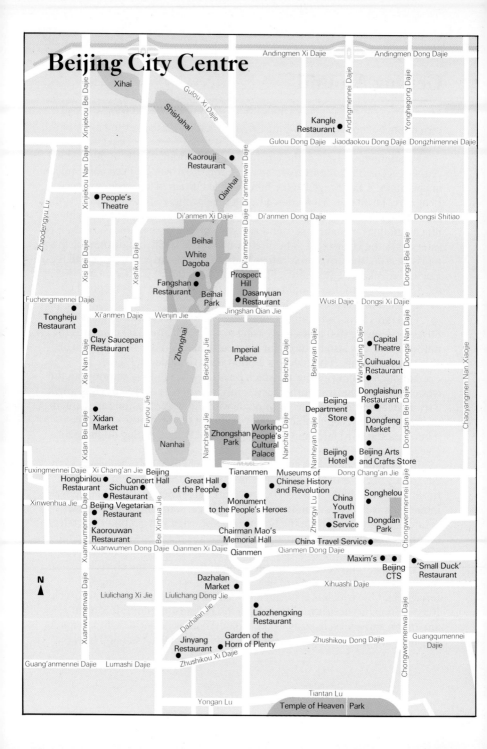

Beijing City Centre

Andingmen Xi Dajie
Andingmen Dong Dajie

Xihai

Gulou Xi Dajie

Xinjiekou Bei Dajie

Shishahai

Andingmennei Dajie

Yonghegong Dajie

Kangle
Restaurant

Gulou Dong Dajie   Jiaodaokou Dong Dajie   Dongzhimennei Dajie

Xinjiekou Nan Dajie

Kaorouji
Restaurant

Qianhai

Zhaodengyu Lu

People's
Theatre

Di'anmen Xi Dajie
Di'anmen Dong Dajie

Dongsi Shitiao

Di'anmennei Dajie   Di'anmenwai Dajie

Xisi Bei Dajie

Xishiku Dajie

Beihai

White
Dagoba

Prospect
Hill

Dongsi Bei Dajie

Fuchengmennei Dajie

Fangshan
Restaurant

Beihai
Park

Dasanyuan
Restaurant

Wusi Dajie

Dongsi Xi Dajie

Tongheju
Restaurant

Xi'anmen Dajie

Wenjin Jie

Jingshan Qian Jie

Clay Saucepan
Restaurant

Zhonghai

Beichang Jie

Imperial
Palace

Beichizi Jie

Beiheyan Dajie

Wangfujing Dajie

Capital
Theatre

Cuihualou
Restaurant

Dongsi Nan Dajie

Xisi Nan Dajie

Xidan Bei Dajie

Fuyou Jie

Donglaishun
Restaurant

Chaoyangmen Nan Xiaojie

Xidan
Market

Nanhai

Nanchang Jie

Zhongshan
Park

Working
People's
Cultural
Palace

Nanchizi Jie

Nanheyan Dajie

Beijing
Department
Store

Dongfeng
Market

Dongdan Bei Dajie

Fuxingmennei Dajie

Xi Chang'an Jie

Beijing

Tiananmen

Museums of
Chinese History
and Revolution

Dong Chang'an Jie

Beijing
Hotel

Beijing Arts
and Crafts Store

Hongbinlou
Restaurant

Concert Hall

Sichuan
Restaurant

Great Hall
of the People

Zhengyi Lu

China
Youth
Travel
Service

Songhelou

Chongwenmennei Dajie

Xinwenhua Jie

Beijing Vegetarian
Restaurant

Bei Xinhua Jie

Monument
to the People's Heroes

Dongdan
Park

Xuanwumennei Dajie

Kaorouwan
Restaurant

Chairman Mao's
Memorial Hall

China Travel Service

Xuanwumen Dong Dajie

Qianmen Xi Dajie

Qianmen

Qianmen Dong Dajie

Maxim's

'Small Duck'
Restaurant

Beijing
CTS

N

Dazhalan
Market

Xihuashi Dajie

Chongwenmenwai Dajie

Liulichang Xi Jie

Liulichang Dong Jie

Dazhalan Jie

Laozhengxing
Restaurant

Jinyang
Restaurant

Garden of the
Horn of Plenty

Zhushikou Xi Dajie

Zhushikou Dong Dajie

Guangqumennei
Dajie

Guang'anmennei Dajie

Lumashi Dajie

Tiantan Lu

Yongan Lu

Temple of Heaven   Park

Recommended Restaurants

Chinese

Most Chinese restaurants in the west are Cantonese, with a few serving Shanghai or Sichuan food. The typical food of Beijing is rather different. Rice is not grown in north China as abundantly as in the south and the staple cereal is wheat. Steamed bread, dumplings and many kinds of noodles form the basis of any Beijing meal. The most commonly eaten vegetables are those of a northern climate — carrots, spinach, turnips, scallions, or large white cabbages.

Beijing has adopted and modified various northern cooking techniques — particularly for barbecueing or boiling mutton — which are now a special feature of its cuisine. But the capital's most celebrated dish, famous far beyond the borders of China, is Beijing duck. First boiling water is poured over the bird, which is then hung for several hours to dry. The duck is basted with syrup, and air is pumped into it to separate the skin from the layer of fat underneath, so ensuring that the skin is crisped while the bird cooks on a spit. The skin, which is the delicacy, is eaten with small pancakes, scallions and a thick, slightly sweet, sauce. After slices of meat have been eaten, the rest of the bird is often used to make stock for soup, which is served at the end of the meal.

The other famous dish of Beijing is the *shuanyangrou*, usually known in English as the Mongolian hotpot. More suitable for winter than summer, cooking is done at the table in boiling stock contained in a charcoal-burning metal pot with a chimney. The diners themselves plunge finely sliced mutton into the stock, followed by a variety of vegetables, beancurd, and vermicelli.

Beijing has a long-established tradition of possessing excellent restaurants which offer the best of China's many regional cuisines. This reputation is still well justified, and first-class restaurants serve food from Sichuan, Shanxi, Shandong, Qinghai, Canton and Shanghai.

Most foreigners drink Chinese beer or sweet Chinese-produced soft drinks. Chinese wines are mostly quite sweet, although dry grape wines, both red and white, are increasingly available in places where foreigners eat. There are some excellent rice wines, such as Shaoxing, although it is not always available. The highly potent Chinese spirit *maotai*, made from sorghum, is good for any flagging social occasion and is a great stimulus to speechmaking, but it is an acquired taste. Although imported alcohol is not usually served in restaurants, it is possible to buy quite a wide range of imported wines and spirits, as well as Coca-Cola, in hotel shops.

Most of the restaurants listed below are used to preparing set banquets for visitors, served in private rooms. But while a private dining room may be preferable for a special occasion or for large groups, the adventurous diner going out alone, or in a small group, should not be deterred from asking to eat in the same part of the restaurant as the local Chinese.

The quantity of food served at a banquet can sometimes be overwhelming — there may be as many as 15 courses. One way to avoid this is, when booking the meal, to stipulate only five or six courses and a low price per head. Banquet prices in Beijing generally range from Rmb50–150 a head, depending on the restaurant. Restaurants tend to close very early in Beijing. It is almost always necessary to book in advance. A CITS guide or hotel staff can help you to do this.

With the opening of international-standard hotels has come a wave of new top-quality Chinese restaurants. Although perhaps not as exciting as dining out in a local restaurant, these hotels offer some of the best Chinese food in the city, with polished service to match. For Cantonese food (prepared under the professional eye of Hong Kong chefs), you could try the **Four Seasons** at the Jianguo (tel. 5002233) which serves a particularly good *dim sum* (11:30 am–2 pm); the Jinglun's **Tao Li**, which specializes in both Cantonese and Chaozhou dishes (tel. 5002266), the **Fan** at the Great Wall Sheraton (tel. 5005566), the new **Spring Garden** at the Holiday Inn Lido (tel. 5006688), and the refined **Shang Palace** at the Shangri-la (tel. 8021122). The Great Wall Sheraton's **Yuan Tai** offers classic Sichuan delicacies, together with a splendid panoramic view from the 22nd floor of the hotel.

Beijing

Clay Saucepan (Shaguoju)
60 Xisi Nan Dajie
tel. 661126

沙锅居
西四南大街60号

This is the oldest restaurant in Beijing, claiming a history which goes back some 300 years. Perhaps the best known all-pork restaurant in Asia, it is said to have originated as a shop selling off pigs that the emperor had sacrificed for a good harvest. An all-pork banquet can be ordered in advance, or it is possible to try just a few of the famous dishes, such as deep fried pork liver or fried pork ribs, along with various soups and vegetable dishes.

Donglaishun
16 Donghuamen, at the north entrance of Dongfeng Market
tel. 550069

This is an excellent place to try Mongolian hotpot in unpretentious surroundings with pleasant service. Highly popular with the people of Beijing, this restaurant is always busy. The lamb shashlik — chunks of lamb rolled in sesame seed and barbecued — is specially good, and for the more

东来顺饭店
东华门16号

adventurous there are other Mongolian specialities to try such as braised camel's hump or camel tendons.

Fangshan
Beihai Park tel. 442573

仿膳饭店
北海公园

This prestigious restaurant uses recipes from the 19th-century imperial Court. Banquets are highly elaborate and expensive — a meal including delicacies such as sharksfin and bird's nest soup might cost over Rmb100 a head. When the restaurant first opened in the '20s it was considered to be the best in Beijing, although today some westerners find the food over-rich and indigestible. But with a magnificent setting on an island in the centre of the beautiful lake in Beihai Park, this must surely rank as one of the most splendid restaurants in China.

Kangle
259 Andingmennei
Dajie tel. 443884

康乐餐馆
安定门内大街259号

Although the food at the Kangle is predominantly northern, the restaurant is famous for its dishes from Yunnan, the province in the far southwest of China. The best-known dish here is called 'crossing the bridge noodles' — noodles cooked in chicken stock. There are several versions of how the dish acquired its intriguing name. One claims that noodles which were destined for the emperor's table were dropped into a pot of boiling water at the bridge which led into the Imperial Palace. By the time the pot had reached the table, the noodles were exactly ready to be served up. Try some of the excellent soups that are served here, as well as the delicious Yunnan chicken, steamed in oil and delicately flavoured with herbs.

Kaorouji
14 Shishaqianhai
Dong Yan tel. 445921

北京烤肉店
什刹前海东沿14号

This small and sometimes expensive restaurant specializing in Mongolian barbecued lamb is sought out by discriminating visitors. Situated just north of Beihai Park, the restaurant has a balcony which looks out over an interesting local neighbourhood and a small lake. In the warmer months it is worth booking well in advance to make sure of a table on the balcony.

Pavilion for Listening to the Orioles (Tingliguan)
Yiheyuan tel. 281936

听鹂馆
颐和园

Beijing Duck Restaurants (Beijing Kaoya Dian)

北京烤鸭店

'Sick Duck' (Wangfujing Kaoya Dian)
13 Shuaifuyuan
tel. 553310

王府井烤鸭店
师府园13号

'Small Duck' (Pianyifang Kaoya Dian)
2 Chongwenmenwai
Dajie tel. 750505

便宜坊烤鸭店
崇文门外大街 2 号

In attractive rooms round a courtyard in the heart of the Summer Palace, this lunch restaurant is very popular with western visitors. The food is an eclectic mixture of different Chinese styles, all of the dishes appealing to foreigners. Try the deep fried steamed bread and the fresh fish from the Summer Palace's Kunming Lake.

A Beijing duck banquet may consist of far more than just the serving of the crisp skin and meat of the tender bird, accompanied by pancakes, sesame buns, scallions and thick brown fermented sauce. Cold duck dishes — which may include meat in aspic, shredded webs, and sliced liver — are usually served first, followed by fried duck heart, liver and gizzard, and the delicious duck soup which comes at the very end of the meal.

Most visitors to Beijing want to try the famous duck dinner and, as a result, the branches of the official Beijing Duck Restaurant tend to turn out rather routine meals. Opinions vary on the best place to go to sample Beijing duck, but many would favour the small restaurant off Wangfujing, known locally as the 'Sick Duck' because of its proximity to the Capital Hospital. Other branches are the 'Small Duck', the 'Big Duck', the 'Super Duck' (a four-storey modern building that can seat about 2000 people at one time) and the 'Jianguomen Duck'. The fifth, near the Jianguo Hotel, is a new venture by the Beijing branch of CITS. You can get a duck banquet for any number without reservation. Although the restaurant is open until midnight, the last duck order is taken at 7:30 pm.

(Previous page and below) A variety of cuisines can be enjoyed in Beijing, including elaborate banquets, imperial-style

45

'Big Duck' (Qianmen Kaoya Dian)
24 Qianmen Dajie
tel. 751379

前门烤鸭店
前门大街24号

'Super Duck' (Heping Kaoya Dian)
Xuanwumen Dajie
tel. 334422

和平烤鸭店
宣武门大街

Jianguomen Duck (Jianguomen Kaoya Dian)
10 Jianguomenwai
Dajie tel. 5002567

建国门烤鸭店
建国门外10号

Ritan Park Restaurant
Ritan Park tel. 592648

日坛公园饭店
日坛公园

This little restaurant in the heart of the Temple of the Sun Park is located in a delightful old courtyard, and it is possible to eat outside when the weather permits. It is popular with the foreign resident community of Beijing for its very good *jiaozi* — steamed dumplings.

Cantonese

Dasanyuan
50 Jingshan Xi Jie
tel. 445378

大三院
京山西街50号

Outside the joint-venture hotels, this is one of the few authentic Cantonese restaurants in Beijing and is quite pricey. Meat and vegetables are brought in daily from Guangdong Province to supply the restaurant with its many specialities, which include roast suckling pig, dog meat, seafood, chicken cooked in tea, turtle meat and special seasonal dishes such as 'battle between the dragon and the tiger' — cat meat with three kinds of snake — and crab and giant salamander.

Moslem

Hongbinlou
82 Xi Chang'an Jie
tel. 336461

鸿宾楼
西长安街82号

This long-established Moslem restaurant, serving no pork, has been open for nearly a century, and continues to specialize in some of Beijing's favourite dishes — Beijing duck, Mongolian hotpot, and pieces of lamb barbecued on skewers — but its wide menu includes many other famous dishes well worth trying, such as sliced sautéed eel, and chicken breasts in red sauce.

Huimin Kaorouwan
102 Xidan Nan,
Xuanwumen
tel. 330700

回民烤肉丸
宣武门西单南102号

Serving a variety of Moslem-style dishes, this restaurant's speciality is barbecued mutton. This dish is particularly enjoyable during the winter, when you may stand around special barbecue stoves and cook the thin strips of mutton yourself, adding noodles, onions and eggs as you like.

Jenghiz Khan Restaurant
Anjialou, Liangmaqiao
Lu tel. 471617

成吉思汗酒家
亮马桥安家楼

The enterprising owner of a small inn for Mongolian travellers coming to Beijing had the bright idea of setting up this authentic Mongolian restaurant in two yurts; one has low Mongolian-style seating and the other regular seating. The traditional menu includes leg of lamb, kebabs, even whole lamb, as well as Mongolian hotpot and boiled duck — all served by staff in Mongolian dress. A meal costs between Rmb30–80 a head. Set out on a dusty road, northeast from the Great Wall Sheraton, this is definitely a restaurant for adventurous eaters. It has quickly become a favourite with the expatriate community and reservations are essential.

Qinghai

Qinghai Restaurant
555 Dongsi Bei Dajie
tel. 442947

青海餐厅
东四北大街555号

The speciality of this restaurant is 'chicken with caterpillars' — chicken stuffed with a fungus found in the distant western Chinese province of Qinghai which is called 'winter worm, summer grass' — and looks exactly like a small caterpillar. Dog meat and shashliks are also served here.

Shandong

Cuihualou
60 Wangfujing
tel. 554561

萃华楼
王府井60号

A popular and long established restaurant serving Shandong-style food. Among its specialities is 'peach flower rice' — crispy-rice over which is poured, in front of you at the table, a sweet and sour prawn sauce, so that it hisses and pops and must be eaten quickly before the rice turns soggy.

**Garden of the Horn
of Plenty
(Fengzeyuan)**
83 Zhushikou Xi Dajie
tel. 332828

丰泽园
珠市口西大街83号

One of Beijing's most famous eating houses, the Fengzeyuan is celebrated for its Shandong food. The cuisine of this coastal province south of Beijing includes some excellent fish dishes. Particulary well known here is the sea cucumber, soup with cuttle-fish eggs, and braised fish with a rich brown sauce. The restaurant enjoys a high reputation, and banquets here are invariably good.

Hongxinglou
1 Beiwei Lu
tel. 332015, 334158

鸿星楼
北纬路 1 号

This restaurant serves typical north China cuisine and, besides a repertoire of 200 Shandong provincial dishes, also boasts of 20 different kinds of *jiaozi* — steamed dumplings with tasty fillings; try their *guo tie* — steamed dumplings which have been lightly fried.

Tongheju
3 Xisi Nan Dajie
tel. 660925

同和居
西四南大街 3 号

Another Shandong-style restaurant with private dining rooms off a small courtyard in the northwestern part of the city. Seafood specialities include sea cucumber, 'squirrel fish' in sweet sauce, jumbo prawns in various styles, and crab and eel in season. Steamed white bread rolls are popular here and their dessert is famous throughout Beijing — 'three non sticks' — an elusively flavoured but delicious custard, made from egg yolks and cornflour with an extra-ordinary texture — whence its name comes — 'won't stick to your plate, won't stick to your chopsticks and won't stick to your mouth.'

Shanxi

Jinyang
241 Zhushikou Xi
Dajie tel. 331669

晋阳饭店
珠市口西大街241号

This interesting restaurant in the southern section of the city is in the house formerly used by Mei Lanfang (1894–1961), the most famous of all Beijing opera actors, for his National Theatre Study Group. The finest rooms in the house now serve as impressive dining rooms. The kitchens specialize in the cuisine of Shanxi — the province to the west of Beijing. This is the perfect setting to try the delicious crisp duck of Shanxi — to some western palates preferable to the rich Beijing duck.

Sichuan

Sichuan
51 Rongxian Hutong
tel. 336356

四川饭店
绒线胡同51号

This elegant restaurant in attractive traditional old buildings with dining rooms arranged round a series of courtyards is the most famous Sichuan restaurant in China, specializing in the hot spicy cuisine of the large southwestern province. Any of the many specialities here is worth trying. The smoked duck, spiced beancurd, and braised eggplant have been specially recommended. For those who do not want every course to be highly seasoned, it is possible to ask the kitchen to make some milder dishes.

Suzhou

Songhelou
10 Taijichang Jie
tel. 555222, 555548

松鹤楼菜馆
台基厂大街10号

The original Songhelou was in Suzhou, where it specialized in the delicate, tender, slightly sweet cuisine of the city, which was particularly favoured by Emperor Qianlong. Recommended in the Beijing restaurant are dishes typical of the Suzhou area — squirrel-shaped mandarin fish, beggar's chicken, turtle with white sauce, Tai Lake greens soup, and winter mushrooms with bamboo shoots. Songhelou's banquet rooms are modelled on the original Suzhou restaurant.

Vegetarian

Beijing Vegetarian Restaurant
74 Xuanwumennei
Dajie tel. 334296

北京素香斋
宣武门内大街74号

The Chinese are masters at the art of vegetarian cooking, and are capable of producing an astonishing variety of dishes from the versatile beancurd, which forms the basis of their vegetarian food. The restaurant can provide a well-balanced banquet of as many as 15 dishes that seem like pork, duck or fish, together with fresh vegetables, many different kinds of mushrooms and seaweed, steamed dumplings and noodles.

Japanese

The rapidly growing population of Japanese residents in the capital has spawned a number of good new Japanese restaurants, several of them in hotels. The Japanese restaurant in the **Beijing Hotel** is well worth trying, the one in the **Xinqiao** less so, but the **Jianguo**'s Japanese restaurant is reputed to be amongst the best in town. A joint venture with Nakabachi of Tokyo, it is small, very expensive, and has an authentic feel to it — staff were well trained in Japan, and the bulk of the equipment, expertise and ingredients are imported. Reservations are essential.

Duoweizhai
Xinyuanli

多味斋
新源里

Amongst Japanese businessmen Duoweizhai has the reputation of being the best Japanese restaurant in town. The chefs are Japanese, the waiters wear traditional dress, and the extensive menu covers sushi, sashimi, teriyaki, sukiyaki, tempura, with an impressive range of appetizers and numerous kinds of sake. Traditional private rooms with floor-seating may be booked. The restaurant is rather large and animated, lacking the intimacy of traditional Japanese restaurants. It is open for lunch 11:30 am−2 pm, and stays open late by Beijing standards for dinner from 5:30 pm to midnight.

Baiyun Guesthouse
Youhao Guesthouse, 7 Houyuanensi, Jiaodaokou, tel. 441036

This intimate restaurant is in a charming setting, down a secluded *hutong*, and is part of the Youhao Guesthouse complex where Chiang Kai-Shek used to live when he visited Beijing. The quiet courtyard, gardens and fountain create a tranquil

白云宾馆
友好宾馆交道口后园
恩寺7号

atmosphere that is unusual in modern Beijing. The restaurant serves fresh sushi, sashimi, seafood tempura, as well as teriyaki, tempura and sukiyaki. It is open every evening 6–11 pm except Mondays.

Western

The new foreign-managed hotels, with European chefs heading up the kitchen staff, have greatly improved the standard of western cooking in the capital. Just five years ago, it was almost impossible to find acceptable — sometimes even recognizable — western food. Although none of Beijing's western restaurants can match Hong Kong's best, all the new foreign-managed hotels have good (but not gourmet) European restaurants, with pleasant service, and a palatable, although not extensive, wine list. (Wine prices are very high, largely because of hefty import duties.) For many foreign visitors to China, dining in a soft-lit leisurely atmosphere makes a welcome change from the austere and hurried mood of many Chinese restaurants. Because so many of the ingredients still have to be imported, as well as the staff to prepare them, you should expect to pay a lot for a European meal.

At the Great Wall Sheraton is the elegant **La France**, and at the Holiday Inn Lido, the **Marco**, which also has a good lunchtime buffet. Many regular visitors to Beijing favour **Justine's** in the Jianguo, where you may dine by candlelight in the evenings. A pleasant alternative is **Dynasty**, the European restaurant in the next-door Jinglun. This is also becoming a firm favourite with business visitors and expatriates. Make reservations early for all these. The joint-venture hotels make special efforts for Sunday lunches or brunches, and the Holiday Inn's Friday evening curry buffet on the **Patio** has become something of an institution. Food promotions are usually advertised in *China Daily*.

International-style coffee shops have also appeared in Beijing. For genuine international coffee shop fare, try the Jinglun, Jianguo, Great Wall Sheraton, Holiday Inn Lido or Shangri-la. Long queues tend to form at peak breakfast, lunch and dinner times, but, under the watchful eye of Hong Kong Chinese managers, the service is good at all of them — by China's standards, at least.

Of the Chinese-run hotels, the best European food is to be had at the **Minzu**, where the revamped ground-floor restaurant has some specialities that match their much more expensive foreign-run counterparts. For a Chinese version of western fast food, try **Minim's** (underneath Maxim's) at 2 Qianmen Dong Dajie.

Exhibition Centre Restaurant (Beijing Zhanlanguan Fandian)
Xizhimenwai Daijie
tel. 893713

北京展览馆饭店
西直门外大街

Known as the 'Moscow' when it first opened in 1954, this is an interesting legacy of the Russian presence in Beijing. With its immense dining room and high ceilings, the restaurant's severe decor is evocative of the Russian architecture of the '50s. And the wide European menu still retains a strong Slavic flavour. Caviar (a Chinese variety but quite palatable), bortsch, and excellent chicken Kiev served in generous portions, are all worth trying.

Maxim de Pékin
2 Qianmen Dong Dajie
tel. 5122110
(reservations),
5121992 (bar)

北京马克西姆
前门东大街 2 号

Modelled on Maxim's in Paris, the flamboyant art deco interiors, with elaborate use of stained glass and mirrors, seem more outrageous in a Beijing setting than the originals do at the Paris Maxim's.

Owned by Pierre Cardin, this restaurant astonished the city when it first opened in 1983, not just because of its decor, but also on account of the apparently genuine French cuisine, the polished service, and the very high prices. Now, with the appearance of several other quality European restaurants in new hotels, Maxim's is less of a curiosity. Prices have levelled out, and the restaurant is well patronized by diplomats, expatriates and business visitors who like to entertain high-ranking officials there. The menu reads as a Maxim's menu should — Fois Gras de Canard fait Maison, Crêpes Fourrées Suzette, Mousse Glacée Frambôise, Iced Soufflé Grand Marnier, Escargots Fricassée. The wine list is good by Beijing standards. It is open for lunch at 12 noon (when a businessmen's set lunch is offered), and for dinner at 7 pm, closing when the last guests leave. After 9 pm, you may go just for drinks at the bar, where there is a small dancefloor.

Windows-on-the-World
28th−29th Floors,
CITIC Building,
Jianguomenwai
tel. 502255

世界之窗
国际大厦

Opened late in 1985, Windows-on-the-World is perched on the top two floors of the new CITIC International Building where most foreign representative offices are housed. Efficiently run by a team of Hong Kong professionals, this joint-venture comprises a competitively-priced coffee shop (where the businessman's buffet lunch is much in demand), a European restaurant, one of Beijing's best Cantonese restaurants, and a sky-lounge with a bird's eye view of the city. It is much used by business visitors, since there are also meeting rooms and private dining rooms.

Corner Beer Shops

Those cylindrical metal canisters which can be seen on trucks anywhere in Beijing are not filled with cooking gas — but with beer. Since it was introduced to China by the British and Germans in the 19th century, beer has become a favourite drink of the people, who regard it as nourishing and healthy, rather than as a stimulant.

On some streets, there are Beijing's own version of 'pubs' — little shops where the canister beer is dispensed under pressure, and side-dishes of sliced kidneys or other snacks are offered at low prices to save people from drinking on an empty stomach.

A glass of beer is a luxury for most Chinese workers, and many of the men enjoying it seem to be pensioners, spinning out a single glass to last an hour or two. Most come on their own, and just sit wrapped in thought as the amber liquid cools their thirst.

Entertainment

Few aspects of Beijing life have changed so dramatically in recent years as the sudden mushrooming of amenities for foreigners. Of course, the city's offerings are still meagre compared with most Asian capitals, but there are more diversions for foreign visitors than five years back when the only evening possibilities were cultural shows, or banquets which tended to wind up before 8 pm. Now Beijing offers (in small quantities) comfortable bars, pleasant restaurants where you can enjoy a leisurely meal, health centres, swimming pools, a 24-hour coffee shop (at the Great Wall Sheraton), even a disco, and a bowling alley.

It is Beijing's new foreign-managed hotels that have been largely responsible for spicing up the capital's leisure time, and this is where the best facilities are to be found.

Nightlife

Beijing's international-style nightlife was pioneered by the Great Wall Sheraton, which got permission to open its plush **Cosmos** nightclub in mid 1984. The club features a specially imported Filipino band — the capital's first. Target clientele is aged 25 upwards, and the municipal ruling that forbids entry to locals is strictly enforced. (Entry Rmb25 Saturday and Sunday, Rmb15 weekdays).

The Holiday Inn Lido has Beijing's first genuinely western-style disco — **Julianna's**. Fitted out by the internationally known Julianna's Sounds System, it looks and sounds like a disco anywhere in the world, with double-sided video screen, imported videos (all passed by the censor), and a British DJ. Very popular with the diplomatic and expatriate community, it fills up fast on Fridays and Saturdays and you should get there early. Again, no locals are allowed in. (Entry Rmb15 at weekends, Rmb10 weekdays.)

To experience a more Beijing-style disco (perhaps more accurately described as dancehall) try the top floor at the **Xiyuan Hotel**, or the back-bar of the **Beijing Hotel**.

Bars

Focal point for Beijing's foreign business community is the friendly **Charlie's Bar** in the Jianguo Hotel. At lunchtime you can eat pleasantly from Charlie's buffet menu and, some evenings, pizzas, tacos and other specialities are on offer. The Jianguo's bustling lobby, where a pianist plays nightly through the general hubbub, is a favourite meeting spot. Another popular meeting place is the **Beijing Hotel**'s ground floor coffee shop, affectionately known as 'the zoo' by regulars who appreciate the interesting mix of clientele and passers-by. For a more elegant, spacious setting (also with musical accompaniment in the evenings) there is little to beat the atrium lobby at the **Great Wall Sheraton**.

For a splendid panorama of the city, there is the **Sky Lounge** at Windows-on-the-World, in the CITIC Building, Jianguomenwai. Or, for a bird's eye view from the northwest of the city, there is the revolving lounge on top of the Xiyuan Hotel, Erligou (although this is not the place if you are after attentive service). Rooftop cafés at the Beijing Hotel, and **Friendship Hotel**, attract lively crowds in the summer.

To escape the hotel circuit, there is **Maxim's** lavishly ornate bar (2 Qianmen Xi Lu), which serves drinks to non-diners after 9 pm and does not close until the last guests leave, no matter how late. There is also a small, sparsely used dance floor here.

Sports

The largest, most pleasant, outdoor pool open to foreigners is at the **Friendship Hotel**. This is open June – September. **Great Wall Sheraton** has a small leisure pool (indoor/outdoor) and a health club, managed by Clark Hatch, open 7 am – 10 pm, complete with gym, sauna, whirlpool and steambaths, as well as aerobics sessions. (For non-residents an all-inclusive entry fee is Rmb36, or less if you select one or two facilities.) Swimming and gym wear may be hired. There are also tennis courts here, as well as massage and acupuncture. (Annual membership is US$400, which gives unlimited use of all sports facilities.) When the **Shangri-la** is fully open in 1987, there will be another top-quality pool and health club in the city.

Chinese massage and acupuncture are, of course, much more widely offered than western-style health facilities in Beijing's hotels, and the charges are more reasonable.

The **Holiday Inn Lido**'s new sports complex (which includes indoor/outdoor tennis courts, jacuzzi, pool, gym, squash, bowling) is the largest in Beijing. This is for members only (tel. 5006688 ext. 2882), but nonresidents may use the heated swimming pool, sauna and health club. The **Fragrant Hills Hotel** also has a good health centre, but it is a long way to travel if you are staying in the city centre.

Holiday Inn Lido has Beijing's only 20-lane automatic AMF **bowling centre** (open 11 am – midnight), equally popular with Beijing's young smart set and the foreign community.

The **International Club**, in Jianguomen, had its heyday when it was one of the few places foreign residents could go. Although clientele has fallen off, the club still has activities for foreign visitors. Its two tennis courts are much in demand, so reserve ahead if you go (tel. 522046). Costs are Rmb30 an hour daytime, Rmb50 an hour at night. There are Chinese and western restaurants at the club, which anyone may use.

For golfers, there is the impressive new **Beijing International Golf Club**, dramatically set in the Ming Tombs area, which opened in mid 1986. A Sino-Japanese joint venture, the course was designed by Japan Golf Promotions, which manages 28 clubs in Japan, and also runs the Zhuhai International Golf Club in Guangdong Province. There is a limited membership of 800 (membership fees were quoted in Japanese yen at Y3,000,000 for individuals, and Y6,000,000 for corporate membership). Individual members may play any day for Rmb17, and corporate members for Rmb60 on weekdays, and Rmb100 at weekends and national holidays. Visitor fees are Rmb120 weekdays, and Rmb200 at weekends and national holidays. Caddie fees are Rmb25, and clubs, shoes and umbrellas may be hired. The luxurious complex includes a clubhouse, reception hall and guesthouse. The city centre contact for the club is at Qianmen Hotel, 1 Yongan Lu, tel. 338731 ext. 4021.

Major spectator sports events are usually held at the **Workers' Stadium** (Gongren Tiyuchang) in the northeast of the city. CITS should be able to tell you what is on, and get tickets. Soccer, table-tennis, basketball, volleyball and, of course, gymnastic events, are the most popular spectator sports.

Performing Arts

Although there is a wide variety of cultural performances in Beijing it is sometimes difficult to find out what is on. There is not always a discernible regularity in performances, nor is there a special 'What's On' publication in English. The visitor simply has to ask around on arrival in the city.

As well as the traditional Chinese arts of opera, music and acrobatics, there is a broadening range of performances of western music, theatre and ballet, along with occasional visits from major foreign performers. Some CITS and CTS staff may tell you which shows are on, and purchase the ticket for you, but others may prove less helpful. A few events are advertised in the English-language *China Daily*.

Buying tickets can be a trying business in Beijing. Tickets for just about everything sell out fast, and some box offices are not keen to sell tickets to foreigners. It is best to try and get someone else to do the queueing for you.

Acrobatics Acrobatic troupes, whose amazing skills derive from a long tradition of street theatre, stage highly sophisticated performances, popular with tourists and locals alike. Many of their best-known acts have a timeless appeal — the 'Pagoda of Bowls', 'Plate Spinning' and 'Handstand upon a Pyramid of Chairs' amongst them. Acrobatics shows may be performed at the **Capital Gymnasium** (Shoudu Tiyuguan), the **Workers' Gymnasium** (Gongren Tiyuchang), and **Beijing Gymnasium** (Beijing Tiyuguan). The city's best-known acrobatics troupes are the China Acrobatics Troupe (Zhongguo Zaji Tuan), which includes animals in its shows, and the Beijing

The Great Wall

Acrobatic Troupe (Beijing Zaji Tuan), but there are other troupes from each district of the city also well worth seeing.

Dance and Music Beijing has two major ballet and opera companies: the Central Opera and Ballet Company (Zhongyang Geju Wuju Tuan) which uses western techniques and has a predominantly western repertoire, and the China Opera and Ballet Company (Zhongguo Geju Wuju Tuan) which combines Chinese and western styles, creating dance-dramas based on Chinese themes.

Numerous visiting song and dance troupes from the various provinces of China come to the capital. They mostly draw their repertoire from the varied cultural traditions of China's many nationalities. Though authentically costumed, the performers are often Han Chinese and the dances and songs are usually based only loosely on the original ethnic form.

At the **International Club** there is a music or dance performance of some kind most weekday evenings, and western films are shown on Saturday nights. For information, telephone 522188.

Modern plays and translations of foreign works are also staged but are difficult for a non-Chinese-speaking foreigner to follow. But an evening spent at a Chinese musical instrument concert is well worthwhile. *Pipa* (Chinese lute) and flute solos are especially popular.

Beijing Opera Traditional Chinese opera is still one of the most popular forms of entertainment in Beijing. Drawing its origins from the Yuan Dynasty (1279—1368), it has developed into over 350 different regional styles. Beijing opera has its own history of over 150 years and uniquely combines acting, singing, dancing and acrobatic skills with spectacular makeup and colourful costumes. The 'painted face' or *jing* character actors are highly adept in applying paint to their faces. The colours depict the whole range of human emotions of the individual character: red indicates loyalty; yellow is cunning; blue is cruelty; white is treachery; black is ferocity. The actors' exaggerated movements form a mime which substitutes for elaborate scenery. Extravagantly stylized and symbolic, Beijing opera draws enthusiastic Chinese audiences.

Traditional Beijing operatic themes derive from Chinese history and mythology — stories such as 'The True and False Monkey King', 'Orphan of the Zhao Family', and 'The White Snake' make for an interesting evening. If you can get a synopsis of the opera before the performance you will enjoy it more. Performances can be long but there is no objection at all to leaving during an interval.

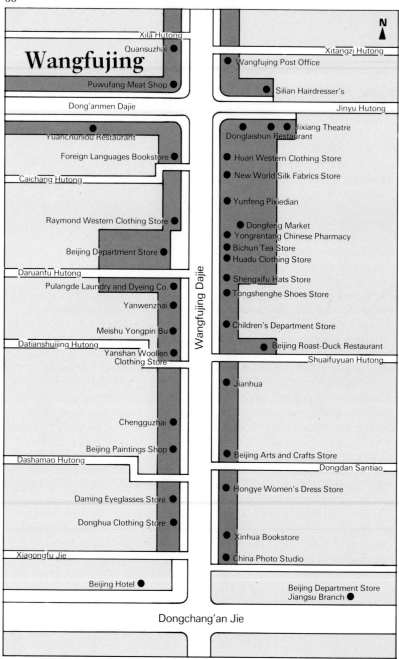

Xila Hutong

Wangfujing

Quansuzhai ●

Puwufang Meat Shop ●

Xitangzi Hutong

● Wangfujing Post Office

● Silian Hairdresser's

Dong'anmen Dajie

Jinyu Hutong

● ● ●Jixiang Theatre
Donglaishun Restaurant

Yuanchunlou Restaurant ●

Foreign Languages Bookstore ●

● Huari Western Clothing Store

● New World Silk Fabrics Store

Caichang Hutong

● Yunfeng Pixiedian

Raymond Western Clothing Store ●

● Dongfeng Market
● Yongrentang Chinese Pharmacy
● Bichun Tea Store
● Huadu Clothing Store

Beijing Department Store ●

● Shengxifu Hats Store

Daruanfu Hutong

● Tongshenghe Shoes Store

Pulangde Laundry and Dyeing Co. ●

Yanwenzhai ●

● Children's Department Store

Meishu Yongpin Bu ●

● Beijing Roast-Duck Restaurant

Datianshuijing Hutong

Shuaifuyuan Hutong

Yanshan Woollen ●
Clothing Store

● Jianhua

Chengguzhai ●

Beijing Paintings Shop ●

● Beijing Arts and Crafts Store

Dashamao Hutong

Dongdan Santiao

● Hongye Women's Dress Store

Daming Eyeglasses Store ●

Donghua Clothing Store ●

● Xinhua Bookstore

Xiagongfu Jie

● China Photo Studio

Beijing Hotel ●

Beijing Department Store
Jiangsu Branch ●

Wangfujing Dajie

N

Dongchang'an Jie

Shopping

Most tourists are anxious to buy something while in Beijing, be it an expensive piece of antique porcelain or simply a small memento of their visit to China's capital city.

Beijing has a number of interesting shops for the visitor to browse in, selling a range of attractive traditional crafts (cloisonné, jade carvings, jewellery, lacquerware, embroidery, painting, silk) which would do well as souvenirs. New shops are flourishing in the hotels and are well worth looking at — especially those at the Beijing Hotel. Department stores are better stocked, and innumerable privately-owned speciality shops are opening up around the city. If you have the time or the inclination to shop around, Beijing offers plenty of scope. As a rule of thumb, buy as soon as you find what you like — you can never be sure to see the same item again.

Free markets give an interesting perspective on Beijing's blossoming consumerism, and you may also find here handicrafts not available in regular stores. Easy to visit would be the free market off Jianguomen (just round the corner from the Jianguo Hotel), or the ones in Sanlihe or at Beitaipingzhuang. Lively night markets thrive in the major shopping areas such as Wangfujing and Xidan, and sell household goods, clothes and food up to 10 pm or even later.

Although Beijing's prices are rising, there are still bargains to be had. Shoppers may discover that merchandise in tourist areas can be found in shops off the tourist route for a much lower price. Some items, however, particularly antiques and carpets, can be more expensive in China than outside (notably in Hong Kong), so if you are planning to buy something special, try and check prices at home beforehand, or in Hong Kong if you are passing through. Bargaining is not accepted in State-owned stores where prices are fixed, but, if handled tactfully, might work in smaller privately-owned establishments.

Stores in Beijing are open seven days a week from 8 or 8:30 am to about 7:30 or 8 pm, and even on the few public holidays many open their doors for business.

The packing and transportation of large, heavy or breakable purchases can be arranged by the Friendship Store, whether the goods to be shipped were bought there or not, but it may be time-consuming, and shipment is expensive. Some of the major new hotels also arrange shipping.

Main Shopping Areas

There are three main shopping areas in the city — Wangfujing, near the Beijing Hotel, Qianmen and Dazhalan, south of Tiananmen Square, and

Liulichang. These areas throng with jostling crowds all day long, and a browse in any of the local shops offers an insight into the life-style of the Beijing resident.

Wangfujing

Beijing's main shopping street is Wangfujing — once called Morrison Street after the famous London *Times* correspondent who lived at no. 98 at the turn of the century. During the Ming and Qing it was an area of smart residences, and, as the foreign legation grew at the end of the 19th century, Wangfujing became a prime area for buying speciality goods.

Today's shops contain a good cross-section of high-quality goods available in the city. It is crowded every day of the week and becomes almost impassable on Sundays, Beijing's main shopping day.

Visitors may spend an interesting hour or so looking around one of the main department stores in city, the **Beijingshi Baihuo Dalou**. There is usually a crush at the counters selling electrical goods, clothing, shoes, household goods and cosmetics. There is a good selection of pure silk, and the speciality sections of the newly renovated top floor are worth a look if only to see what goods are currently in vogue in Beijing. The **Dongfeng (East Wind) Market** just across the road occupies a huge area supplying almost every basic daily need, with several small restaurants. In the last years of the Qing Dynasty the market was a maze of small shops, stalls, restaurants and theatres. At the **Dongdan Food Market** a block east of the Beijing Hotel, fresh vegetables, meat and frozen fish are sold. Plates of pre-cut ingredients to be cooked at home are prepared for the convenience of Beijing's working wives.

One of the more interesting shops in the city is the **Beijing Arts and Crafts Store** at 200 Wangfujing, which stocks the largest selection of Chinese traditional handicrafts. Several floors are open to Beijing shoppers as well as tourists, so prices are very reasonable. The third floor is for tourists only. Among its many items are Chinese papercuts, puppets, lacquer and cloisonné ware, embroidered linen, rattan and bamboo ware, Wuxi clay figures, colourful kites, toys, carvings, art materials and a large selection of traditional combs from Changzhou in Jiangsu Province.

Wangfujing's many speciality shops are shown on the map on page 60, and described in the shopping suggestions section (pages 67–72).

Qianmen and Dazhalan

This general area, south of Tiananmen Square and beyond the Qianmen Gate, is particularly interesting to wander in, and its narrow streets, with charming names like 'Fresh Fish Street', 'Corridor Lane', 'Jewellery Market Street' and 'Large Gatepost Lane' reflect the flavour the area once possess-

ed. Street sellers ply a variety of goods from magazines and hair-rollers to pipes and suitcases, and in winter hot peanuts, chestnuts, sweet potatoes and glasses of tea. Local inns indicate the area's proximity to the railway station and many of the shoppers are from the provinces. Food shops sell local delicacies and Chinese medicine shops offer ginseng roots, fungi and deer antlers, while on the corner of Zhushikou and Qianmen one can watch the art of making bamboo steamers. Dazhalan, once known for its theatres and teashops, is still the home of the Beijing Acrobatic Troupe rehearsal house and is a busy shopping street.

Liulichang

The charming old street known as Liulichang (Glazed Tile Factory) is Beijing's best-known shopping street for good quality antiques, books and paintings. It has been completely restored, and the high concentration of shops, many privately-owned, make it an attractive place to wander in, even if you do not intend to buy anything.

Liulichang was established over 500 years ago in the Ming Dynasty. Initially it was the site of a large factory which made glazed tiles for the Imperial Palace. Gradually other smaller tradesmen began to cluster around, and at the beginning of the Qing, many booksellers moved there. The area became a meeting place for intellectuals and a prime shopping district for art objects, books, handicrafts and antiques.

In 1949 Liulichang still had over 170 shops, but many were quickly taken over by the State. Inevitably, much of the street was ransacked during the Cultural Revolution. Large-scale renovation of the traditional architecture has only just been completed. The street is divided into east and west sections (see map on page 65). Some of the best shops are detailed in the merchandise sections, pages 67–73.

Free Markets

Visitors interested in looking at a free market could try the one located along the northeastern wall of the Temple of Heaven. Goods can include grains and pulses, peanuts, vegetables, pheasants, orchid and peony plants, dried tobacco leaves and fresh crabs in season. Sofas and chairs are in great demand and can be seen being loaded precariously across a bicycle by the happy new owner. Painters and calligraphers display their work and write auspicious marriage inscriptions on red paper upon request.

The **Guanyuan Market**, which specializes in birds and fish, is also worth a visit. It is a small, crowded spot in the northwest of the city, opposite Guanyuan Park, where Beijing's bird-lovers and goldfish fanciers gather to admire and purchase singing birds — thrushes, mynahs, canaries, budgies and Beijing robins — carved bamboo cages, tiny porcelain seed and water bowls, and bird-food, including live grasshoppers and long fat worms. Fish breeders defend their enamel basins of colourful fish from the crush of on-lookers. Sometimes turtles, squirrels or guinea-pigs can be found there. Sunday is the best day to visit this market.

The Friendship Store

Friendship Stores were established to sell to foreigners export goods which were not available to local people. Nowadays some items on sale in Friendship Stores can be bought elsewhere, but the range and quality of goods is sometimes better — and the prices often higher.

Liulichang

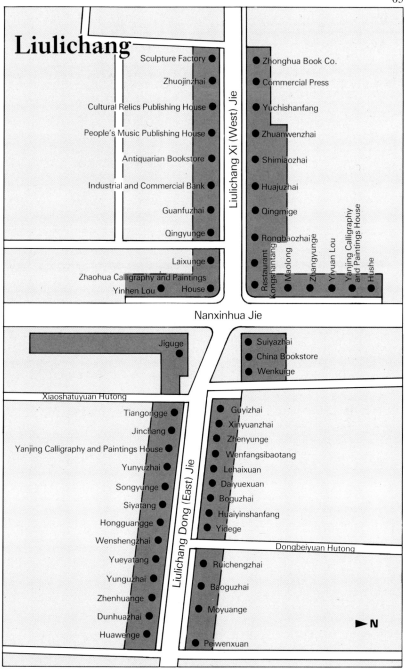

Sculpture Factory ●

Zhuojinzhai ●

Cultural Relics Publishing House ●

People's Music Publishing House ●

Antiquarian Bookstore ●

Industrial and Commercial Bank ●

Guanfuzhai ●

Qingyunge ●

Laixunge ●

Zhaohua Calligraphy and Paintings House ●

Yinhen Lou ●

Liulichang Xi (West) Jie

● Zhonghua Book Co.

● Commercial Press

● Yuchishanfang

● Zhuanwenzhai

● Shimiaozhai

● Huajuzhai

● Qingmige

● Rongbaozhai

Restaurant Kongshantang ●
Maolong ●
Zhangyunge ●
Yivuan Lou ●
Yanjing Calligraphy and Paintings House ●
Hushe ●

Nanxinhua Jie

Jiguge ●

● Suiyazhai

● China Bookstore

● Wenkuige

Xiaoshatuyuan Hutong

Tiangongge ●

Jinchang ●

Yanjing Calligraphy and Paintings House ●

Yunyuzhai ●

Songyunge ●

Siyatang ●

Hongguangge ●

Wenshengzhai ●

Yueyatang ●

Yunguzhai ●

Zhenhuange ●

Dunhuazhai ●

Huawenge ●

Liulichang Dong (East) Jie

● Guyizhai

● Xinyuanzhai

● Zhenyunge

● Wenfangsibaotang

● Lehaixuan

● Daiyuexuan

● Boguzhai

● Huaiyinshanfang

● Yidege

Dongbeiyuan Hutong

● Ruichengzhai

● Baoguzhai

● Moyuange

● Peiwenxuan

► N

The Beijing Friendship Store on Jianguomenwai Daije has a particularly vast choice of merchandise. Shopping here is easier than in the crowded department stores, and some of the shop assistants speak English. A branch of the Bank of China is located on the second floor which will change foreign currency, travellers cheques and honour most well-known credit cards.

The ground floor (first floor Chinese-style) sells an amazing combination — meat, vegetables, canned foods, cigarettes, wine and spirits, sweets, fresh flowers, TV sets, Chinese medicine, carpets, bicycles, furniture and goldfish — principally for the consumption of the many foreign residents of Beijing. The second floor is devoted to clothing. A wide range of beautiful pure silk, Shandong silk, raw silk, brocades and cotton is well displayed. Cashmere sweaters and cardigans are reasonably priced and of very good quality. Suede and leather jackets and coats and a selection of furs are also on sale. Traditional Chinese silk padded jackets are popular, as are the comfortable black cotton shoes, while silk embroidered blouses for women come in numerous styles and soft colours. There are several tailors, but since they are usually busy with the needs of residents it is unlikely that they would be able to complete anything in a short time.

Jewellery, handicrafts, embroideries, table linen, antique and modern porcelain, ivory, jade, wood and stone carvings, coromandel screens and lacquerware are among the wealth of traditional items to choose from on the third floor.

Shopping Suggestions

Antiques

Antiques which can be exported must bear a red seal, although the red seal does not guarantee that an item is necessarily an antique worthy of the name. On the whole, the oldest pieces date from the middle to late Qing period — between 100 and 120 years old. Many pieces sold as antiques may be no more than 50 or 60 years old, but the shop assistants are truthful about the period of any particular item, when asked. The **Yueyatang** in the Beijing Hotel is the exception. Here it is possible to purchase much older objets d'art, such as Ming porcelain, Tang carvings, Zhou coins, and very old paintings and calligraphy.

Most antiques for sale already have a red export seal on them — be sure to keep these on, as you may be required to show the items as well as the receipts to customs on departure. Should you buy antiques which do not have a seal, it is advisable to have one fixed. This involves a visit to the Beijing Arts Objects Clearance Office situated in the compound of the Friendship Store, open 2—5 pm on Mondays and Fridays. A small fee per piece is charged.

The best-known antique shops in Beijing are in Liulichang. **Yunguzhai**, at 80 Liulichang East, is famous for its antique ceramics — vases, plates, bowls, bird-feeds and jars, bronzes and stone Buddhist carvings as well as jade and ivory carvings.

Huaxia Arts and Crafts, 293 Wangfujing, has a small but good collection of porcelain, cloisonné and other small pieces.

On Zhushikou Dajie, just opposite the Fengzeyuan Restaurant, is another shop, the **Zhenyunge**, which has antique porcelain vases, pots and dishes, lacquer boxes, cloisonné, jewellery and miscellaneous objects of interest.

Another shop of particular interest is the **Beijing Arts and Crafts Trust Company** at 12 Chongwenmennei Dajie. Foreign residents call this store the 'Theatre Shop' because of its collections of old Beijing opera gowns and costumes. Although not strictly an antique store, the assortment is fascinating. The first floor has sections selling embroidered linen, old fur coats, carpets and restored pieces of old Chinese furniture. Upstairs are elaborate blue kingfisher-feather hairpins, children's silver pendants, brass ink-boxes and incense burners, Buddhist rosary beads, small old pieces of embroidery and braid and odd pieces of pure kitsch of Chinese, Russian, Japanese or European origin.

Books

The **Foreign Languages Bookstore**, 219 Wangfujing, stocks books in a number of languages printed by Beijing's Foreign Languages Press, as well as some foreign paperbacks, guidebooks and news magazines. Art books on many aspects of China's culture and her treasures are handsomely reproduced. Translations of Chinese novels and short stories, both modern and classical, are most reasonably priced, as are dictionaries and booklets on a wide range of subjects.

The two-storey **Xinhua Bookshop** at 214 Wangfujing is the largest bookstore in Beijing. Long queues form when some new publication or popular reprint comes on sale. The books, all in Chinese, cover most subjects including languages, literature, technology, sciences and history. On the second floor are some excellent art books, and inexpensive reproductions of paintings. There is a counter selling political posters and portraits of Chinese leaders.

The **Friendship Store** has a good collection of newspapers and magazines, and the better hotels also carry a selection of foreign paperbacks, guidebooks, maps, as well as newspapers.

For the sinologist in search of old or specialized books, the best place to go is Liulichang, where there are several antiquarian bookshops (see map page 65). The best collection of art books in Liulichang is at **Zhaohua Calligraphy and Paintings House**, 4 Liulichang West.

From time to time secondhand foreign-language books of interest may be found in the **Dongfeng Market** (see page 62) further down the street.

Carpets

Chinese carpets of all sizes, in classical and contemporary designs in wool and silk, may be seen at the **Friendship Store** (see page 64) and at the carpet pavilion in the Round City at the entrance to Beihai Park. The **Marco Polo Shop** at the Temple of Heaven has old Tianjin (Tientsin) and Central Asian carpets. **Beijing Arts and Crafts**, 200 Wangfujing, also has a good collection of both Chinese and Central Asian carpets, but prices are high. Prices at **Jinchang**, in 118 Liulichang East, are marginally better than at the Friendship Store and Beijing Arts and Crafts.

Embroidery

The **Yuanlong Gu Embroidery Silk Store**, near the north gate of the Tiantan, has a history of more than 80 years and stocks various kinds of silk garments — pyjamas, padded silk jackets, trouser suits and brocade fur coats. It specializes in embroideries from Suzhou — intricate and colourfully embroidered Mandarin jackets, kimonos and blouses, as well as table linen, can be purchased. The store's tailors will make up shirts and blouses at a reasonable price.

Furniture

Tourists interested in Chinese furniture, screens and lacquer cabinets should visit the **Marco Polo Shop** at the Temple of Heaven. Special orders can also be placed here. At 56 Wangfujing there is the **Restored Furniture Shop**, specializing in refinished pieces — campaign desks, grey-marble topped tables, carved chairs and vanity boxes. A similar selection is available at the **Beijing Arts and Crafts Trust Company** (see page 68). Plainer Ming-style chests and cupboards with attractive brass fittings, upright chairs and cabinets are to be found at the **Donghuamen Furniture Shop**, 38 Dongsinan Dajie. Most of these pieces are old and have been restored in the workshop behind the store.

Furs

Apart from the **Friendship Store** (see page 64), the **Jianhua Fur and Leather Store**, 182 Wangfujing, has ready-made fur, leather and suede jackets and coats, or will make them to order. Mink, fox, ermine, sheepskin, rabbit and astrakhan are usually in stock. Some of these skins are bred commercially, others have been hunted.

Jewellery

Modern and traditional styles of jewellery set with semi-precious stones are for sale in many of Beijing's tourist shops. You may find old pieces of silver in the form of pendants which were traditionally worn by children as good-luck charms, small needle-holders which women wore hanging from their jacket-button, pill-boxes, or bells. Chinese skill in cutting and working jade is seen in the artistry of carved figurines, vases and medallions.

Wenfangsibaotang at 99 Liulichang East has a good selection, and **Peiwenxuan** at 37 Liulichang East is a small, charming shop selling attractive antique jewellery and other small trinkets.

Records of medical prescriptions for Emperor Guangxu and Dowager Empress Cixi, Palace Museum Collection

Painting and Calligraphy

The **Beijing Paintings Shop**, 289 Wangfujing, has traditional Chinese paintings, watercolours and calligraphy by modern artists, stone rubbings and woodcut prints. Also in Wangfujing (at 281) is **Chengguzhai**, where paintings may be bought, and **Meishu Yongpin Bu**, at 265, which is a quality dealer in calligraphy, brushes, inks, paper, and silk-covered books. Fan paintings, embroideries, original old scroll paintings and calligraphy by some of China's master painters are found in the famous **Baoguzhai**, in picturesque premises at 63 Liulichang West.

A favourite shop is **Rongbaozhai** at 19, Liulichang West. Here reproductions of old paintings, rubbings and the works of modern painters may be found. This shop specializes in art materials, and its clients are mostly artists, amateur or professional, who lovingly feel the quality of the reams of handmade paper and discuss the merits of the squirrel-hair brush as opposed to the fox-hair brush. Decorative blocks of ink are for sale as are the various porcelain accoutrements of Chinese painting. Behind the shop are artists' workshops well worth taking a look at.

Moyuange, at 61 Liulichang East, is another good shop for paintings, and **Daiyuexuan Hubihuimodian**, at 91 Liulichang East, is a specialist dealer in the 'four essentials' of Chinese calligraphy: paper, ink, brush, inkstone.

Porcelain

While wandering about the streets the visitor will find many small local shops stocking cheap, everyday porcelain and pottery, rice bowls, storage pots and small ornaments which are often quite appealing. In Qianmen Dajie are two shops selling modern porcelain. The **Hunan Pottery Products Store** (at

99) has tea sets, bowls, plates, vases and ornaments all made in Changsha, capital of Hunan Province. The other, the **Jingdezhen Porcelain Shop** (at 149/151) has products from the principal porcelain centre in China, Jingdezhen in Jiangxi Province. Pottery has been made there since the second century BC and during the Northern and Southern Dynasties (317–589) its porcelain graced the tables of the imperial Court. Both Chinese and western dinner services are for sale in various designs, including the famous blue and white rice pattern. A 94-piece Chinese dinner service is priced from Rmb230 and a 92-piece western dinner service starts at Rmb300, depending on the pattern. Tea sets, plant holders and garden seats are among its other products.

Seals and Inkstones

Inkstones and pairs of antique and modern seals in bronze and stone adorned with delightful figures are sold at **Guanfuzhai** (Liulichang East) or at the **Yanwenzhai Seal Shop**, 261 Wangfujing. Both stores carry an impressive array of sizes and styles. The staff will arrange for your name (in Chinese characters if you like) to be engraved on the seal of your choice. Seals can also be engraved with your own Chinese name at the Dongfeng Market (see page 62).

Other Speciality Shops

The **China Stamp Company**, 28 Donganmen Dajie, just off Wangfujing, sells albums of Chinese stamps and individual sets. Crowds of enthusiastic Chinese stamp collectors gather outside this shop to buy, sell or swap with each other.

For cassettes and records try the **Foreign Languages Bookstore**, 16 Donganmen Dajie, which has both western and Chinese music.

The **Beijing Chopstick Shop**, 160 Xidan Bei Dajie, has a wide selection of chopsticks, some forming sets. Strangely, this shop also specializes in walking-sticks and fans.

At the **Nationalities Friendship Store**, Nationalities Palace (Minzugong), beside the Minzu Hotel, there are handicrafts produced by some of China's minority peoples: embroideries from Yunnan, saddle-bags from Xinjiang, decorated wooden saddles from Inner Mongolia and sets of colourful minority costumes. You can even buy a nomad yurt. The **Dazhalan Hat Shop**, 9 Dazhalan, off Qianmen Dajie, has hats traditionally worn by the Tibetan, Mongol and Central Asian minorities. **Shengxifu Maodian**, 156 Wangfujing, has a wide assortment of Chinese fur hats for Beijing winters.

For silk, there is the **New World Silk Fabrics Store** (Xinshijie), at 118 Wangfujing. If you would like to buy Chinese slippers, try **Yunfeng Pixiedian**, at 122 Wangfujing, or **Tongshenghe Shoes Store** at 158 Wangfujing. (Both these stores sell China's attempts at the latest fashions as well).

There is a large pharmacy of traditional Chinese medicine at 136 Wangfujing — **Yongrentang**.

The **Jiguge**, better known as the 'Copy Shop' at 289 Wangfujing, sells handsome reproductions of pottery tomb figures dating from the Han Dynasty (206 BC – AD 220) and later. Bronze reproductions of museum pieces, copies of wall paintings from the Thousand Buddha Caves at Dunhuang and stone rubbings are available too.

The **Nationalities Musical Instrument Shop**, 104 Qianmen Dajie, not only has Chinese traditional musical instruments such as the two stringed *erhu*, elegant *pipa*, drums and clappers, but also Central Asian longstemmed guitars, tambourines and Tibetan horse-headed banjos. The **Hongsheng Music Shop**, 231 Wangfujing, has classical Chinese and western instruments, including guitars.

Everyday Shopping

There is a small but mouth-watering selection of quality breads, cakes and pastries (they are baked to the Hong Kong Peninsula's own recipes), imported cheeses, and cold cuts at the **Jianguo Hotel's Gourmet Corner**. For the best selection get there early, before everything is snapped up by the growing number of expatriates in the city. The Xinqiao Hotel has opened an excellent new boulangerie called **Rosenbec**, which has French bread, croissants and pastries.

The **Holiday Inn Lido** also has an enticing **delicatessen** counter, as well as Beijing's first western-style supermarket. The shelves of the **Lido Market** are stocked with favourite brands of imported groceries, toiletries, cosmetics, baby food and other household items, from Hong Kong, Japan, Singapore, Europe and USA, together with some of the better Chinese brands (open 8 am – 9 pm). This is the place to stock up on provisions if you are embarking on a long bus or train journey. The **Friendship Store** in Wangfujing also has a number of imported everyday items, geared towards foreign tastes, but, like everywhere else in Beijing, stock does not flow smoothly, and even basic items may disappear from the shelves for months.

A number of hotel stores sell small selections of imported beers, wines and spirits, and Nescafé, even if it is not served in their own dining rooms. Prices vary considerably from hotel to hotel. The Friendship Store has a larger stock of imported wines and spirits.

Monument to the People's Heroes, Tiananmen Square

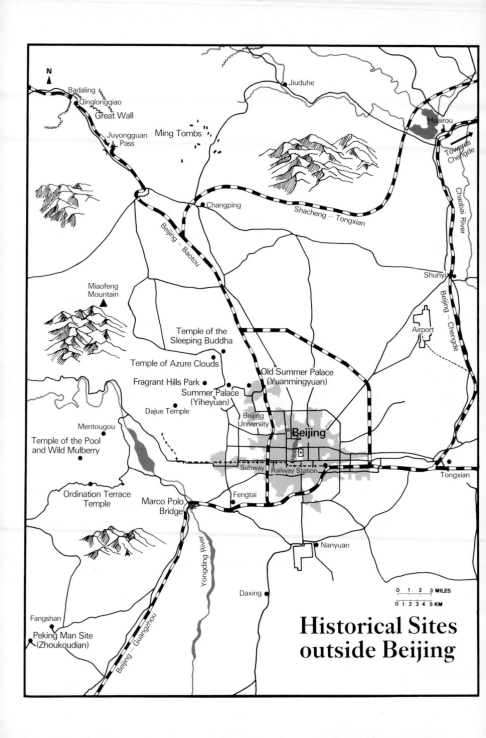

N

Badaling
Qinglongqiao
Great Wall
Juyongguan
Pass

Jiuduhe

Huairou

Towards Chengde

Chaobai River

Ming Tombs

Changping

Shacheng – Tongxian

Beijing – Baotou

Shunyi

Miaofeng
Mountain

Beijing – Chengde

Airport

Temple of the
Sleeping Buddha

Temple of Azure Clouds

Old Summer Palace
(Yuanmingyuan)

Fragrant Hills Park

Summer Palace
(Yiheyuan)

Dajue Temple

Beijing
University

Beijing

Mentougou

Temple of the Pool
and Wild Mulberry

Subway

Railway Station

Tongxian

Ordination Terrace
Temple

Fengtai

Marco Polo
Bridge

Yongding River

Nanyuan

Beijing – Guangzhou

Daxing

0 1 2 3 MILES
0 1 2 3 4 5 KM

Fangshan
Peking Man Site
(Zhoukoudian)

Historical Sites
outside Beijing

History of Beijing

Beijing is both an old and a new city — old in its cultural heritage, and new as the capital of the People's Republic of China whose present leadership is determined to drag her into the 20th century.

So many of the buildings here are steeped in the history of China over the last 800 years, that it becomes rapidly obvious to any visitor how integral the city's development is to the rise and fall of dynasties, and indeed, to Chinese civilization itself.

Peking Man The story of Beijing starts a long time before recorded history. Fragments of the bones of 'Peking Man', dated to a period about 300,000 – 500,000 years ago, were discovered at the village of Zhoukoudian outside the present-day city (see page 121).

Capital of Conquerors During the Zhou (1027 – 221 BC) and subsequent dynasties a series of large established settlements grew around Beijing. But as the area was the focus of an unsettled frontier region far from the capital — Xi'an — and other centres of power further south, it suffered a turbulent history.

For part of the period dominated by the Liao Kingdom (947 – 1125), the city was a secondary capital enjoying the pretty name (which is still used from time to time) of Yanjing, the City of Swallows. In the 12th century the 'Golden Tartars' swept down from Manchuria and wrested the city for their own, newly established, State of Jin.

When Kublai became Great Khan of the eastern part of the Mongol empire in 1260, he decided to develop Beijing as his winter capital, calling it Dadu, or Great Capital, and took up residence in a palace in what is now Beihai Park.

By the time the Venetian explorer Marco Polo reached Beijing at the end of the 13th century, it was called Khanbaliq, the City of the Khan, and was already one of the world's great metropolises. From his long detailed description of the city, it is clear that Marco Polo was utterly overwhelmed by the size and opulence of the Mongol capital.

Under the Ming The Ming Dynasty, founded in 1368 upon the defeat of the Mongols, first established its capital in Nanjing, and on account of its relegation Dadu was renamed Beiping (Northern Peace). With the accession of the dynamic third Ming emperor, Yongle, the dynasty entered a period of vitality and expansion. He re-established Beijing as the capital in 1421, giving the city its modern name, which means Northern Capital, and which Europeans later romanized as Peking.

Much of present-day Beijing was built during the period that immediately followed. In contrast to the unplanned, sprawling cities of the south, traditional concepts of town-planning were employed, and nowhere was this more evident than in the grid layout of Beijing. The foundations of Khan-baliq were, of course, already there, but they were now extended; walls were built and moats were dug. As Beijing flourished, the city originally establish-ed by the Tartars became too small, and in 1553 a new, outer, or Chinese City, wall was built to enclose the suburbs that had burgeoned to the south.

Within the boundaries, a massive building and renovation programme created some of the most striking testimonies to Ming confidence and power. Over 200,000 workmen laboured to build the Imperial Palace be-tween 1407 and 1420. Though the palace buildings have been restored and rebuilt many times since then, the plan remains essentially the same. The Temple of Heaven (a magnificent example of Ming architecture) and the Altar of Agriculture (which no longer exists) were erected in the Outer City. Mindful of their mortality, the early Ming emperors planned and prepared their own burial grounds in the same methodical and grandiose fashion, as can be seen at the Ming Tombs or Shisanling. Nor was the defence of the realm neglected: the Great Wall at Badaling — the section of the wall where visitors are usually taken — was also constructed during this period.

Beijing in the 15th Century

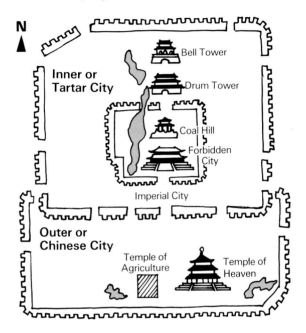

N

Bell Tower

Inner or
Tartar City

Drum Tower

Coal Hill

Forbidden
City

Imperial City

Outer or
Chinese City

Temple of
Agriculture

Temple of
Heaven

Under the Qing For a century after Yongle, stability was maintained in the empire. But weak rulers and corrupt bureaucrats eventually fragmented the authority and drained the energies of the State. The last Ming emperor hanged himself on Prospect Hill behind the Imperial Palace in 1644, when rebels and Manchu forces were already at the city gate.

The Manchus, founders of the Qing (Pure) Dynasty that came to rule China, were descendants of those Tartars who invaded Beijing in the 12th century. This time they were to stay for 267 years.

The Qing were more interested in maintaining the existing capital and administrative systems than in making any radical changes. As they themselves became culturally assimilated (to the extent that they lost their own language), their improvements to Beijing and its environs tended to preserve the styles and techniques of the Ming period. The most interesting contributions the Qing rulers made to their adopted capital were the various summer palaces that they built outside the city.

Notable Qing rulers included Kangxi (reigned 1662–1722), Qianlong (reigned 1736–95) and the Empress Dowager, Cixi (ruled 1861–1908). During the long reigns of the former two, China enjoyed peace and prosperity. The 18th-century European ideal of the Chinese nobility as a highly cultured people dressed in gorgeous silks and much given to splendid ceremonies derived from western travellers' accounts of this land of abundance.

But the ideal was an elaborate facade; the Manchu Court had, by the 19th century, become enervated and stagnant. Clinging rigidly to ancient systems of thought and rituals, the ultra-conservative officials rejected all original ideas or innovations as seditious. Attempts by reformers to modernize China were invariably quashed.

The Coming of the Barbarians The history of the late Qing empire is a sorry account of unsuccessful resistance to western encroachment from without, and to domestic rebellion from within. The First Opium War (1840−42) prised open China to foreign trade. In a second round of the conflict (1858−60), Beijing was actually captured by Britain and France, whose troops burned down the Summer Palaces, and whose representatives established embassies in a Legation Quarter (southeast of the Imperial Palace, in the area bounded by Dong Chang'an Jie, Chongwenmen Jie and the Inner City wall) over which the Chinese had no jurisdiction. It was this legation quarter that the men of 'The Society of the Harmonious Fists', the Boxer rebels, besieged for two months in 1900 in protest against the growing influence of the foreigners.

Piecemeal reforms, reluctantly conceded by Cixi, came too late. Her successor Puyi, who ascended the throne at the age of six, was the last emperor of China. For some years after the collapse of the Qing, he continued to live in the rear quarters of the Imperial Palace, while the front portion was turned into a museum. He finally moved from the palace in 1924.

Under the Republic Following the 1911 Revolution, Beijing became the stage for important events in the development of modern republican China. On 4 May 1919, Tiananmen Square was the arena of an historic mass demonstration: students and patriots, in what became known as the May Fourth Movement, passionately denounced the humiliating terms for China of the newly-signed Treaty of Versailles. It was a show of solidarity that started many Chinese on the road to socialism. In 1928, when the political centre of the Republic was moved to the Nationalists' power base at Nanjing, the old name of Beiping was restored to the abandoned capital. The Nationalist old guard in Taiwan continue to use that name to this day.

Emerging from its Japanese occupation between 1937 and 1945, the city had to wait another four years before regaining its paramount status. The Communists entered Beijing unopposed in January 1949. On 1 October, Chairman Mao Zedong proclaimed the establishment of the People's Republic of China from the rostrum of the Gate of Heavenly Peace, and a new era for Beijing began.

The Changing City In recent years China has once again emerged from her isolation and embarked on a programme of reform. And once more, foreigners have flocked in to do business. As a result of direct investment and joint ventures, international-style hotels and office highrises have sprung up to serve the newcomers to Beijing. So have fast-food stalls and supermarkets. They mingle with the characterless cement blocks that were raised to alleviate the city's housing shortage — accommodating the 10-million population is a chronic problem. Here and there, at street level, the new phenomenon of the *ge ti hu* — individual small-time entrepreneurs — is apparent in the free markets that have mushroomed in, for example, the area north of Dong'anmen Dajie, in bustling Wangfujing.

While much restoration work to historic sites is being undertaken, many major monuments are irretrievably lost, torn down under the post-1949 regime or wantonly destroyed during the Cultural Revolution in the late '60s and early '70s. The signs of progress or western decadence (depending on one's viewpoint) are further changing the appearance of the city. If the impression given by present-day Beijing is of a beautiful old city being defaced by modernization, it is some comfort to recollect that many of its landmarks have managed to survive for several hundred years.

Reigns of Ming and Qing Emperors

Ming Dynasty (1368−1644)

Hongwu	1368−1398
Jianwen	1399−1402
Yongle	1403−1424
Hongxi	1425
Xuande	1426−1435
Zhengtong	1436−1449
Jingtai	1450−1456
Tianshun	1457−1464
Chenghua	1465−1487
Hongzhi	1488−1505
Zhengde	1506−1521
Jiajing	1522−1566
Longqing	1567−1572
Wanli	1573−1620

Taichang	1620
Tianqi	1621−1627
Chongzhen	1628−1644

Qing Dynasty (1644−1911)

Shunzhi	1644−1661
Kangxi	1662−1722
Yongzheng	1723−1735
Qianlong	1736−1795
Jiaqing	1796−1820
Daoguang	1821−1850
Xianfeng	1851−1861
Tongzhi	1862−1874
Guangxu	1875−1908
Xuantong	1909−1911

Sights in Beijing

Tiananmen Square

The enormous square facing the Gate of Heavenly Peace (Tiananmen) is the heart of modern China. During the days of the Qing empire the square did not exist — there were originally buildings on either side of a central thoroughfare leading northwards to the Imperial Palace.

Gradually cleared during the first half of the 20th century, this huge area — it covers about 40 hectares (98 acres) — has witnessed crucial developments in China's history. A number of important political demonstrations took place there during the Republic (1911–49). On 1 October 1949, Chairman Mao proclaimed the establishment of the People's Republic of China from the rostrum of the Gate of Heavenly Peace. Until the middle '70s the square was used to stage massive parades and rallies, but it has also retained its role as a focus for revolutionary protest and dissent. On 5 April 1976, just after Qing Ming — the annual festival on which the Chinese remember their dead — the square was the scene of a riot by angry mobs demonstrating their support for Zhou Enlai, who had died three months earlier. This public mourning for the moderate premier is now seen as a turning point in the political tide, a clear denunciation of the last years of Mao's rule and of Jiang Qing, his widow.

The **Gate of Heavenly Peace** itself is an imposing long red structure with a double roof of yellow tiles on the northern side of the square. On either side of the gate's rear portion are two parks. To the east is the **Working People's Cultural Palace**; over 550 years old, this was an imperial ancestral temple and now contains a park, a library, a gymnasium and other recreational facilities. On the western side is **Zhongshan Park**, dedicated to Dr Sun Yat-sen, the leader of the 1911 Revolution and founder of modern China.

On the eastern side of the square are two major museums, the **Museum of Chinese History** and the **Museum of the Chinese Revolution** (see page 127).

In the centre of the square is the **Monument to the People's Heroes**, an obelisk in memory of those who died for the revolution, with inscriptions by Mao Zedong and Zhou Enlai.

At the far southern end of the square (beyond Chairman Mao's Memorial Hall) is the **Qianmen** or Front Gate, a massive double gate which controlled entry to the northern section of the city.

Great Hall of the People On the western side of the square, this monumental building, completed in 1959, houses the People's Congress. It may usually be visited on Monday, Wednesday and Friday mornings, although opening times may change when party meetings (which naturally take precedence) are scheduled. There is an entrance fee (Rmb5 at the time of writing).

The Great Hall of the People is built round a square, very much in the solid Revolutionary-Heroic mould. It is worth going inside where, even if the decor is not to everyone's taste, the sheer scale of the rooms is breathtaking. From the huge reception room, the Wanren Dalitang (Ten-thousand People Assembly Hall) leads off to the west, the banquet wing to the north, and the offices of the standing committees of the national congress to the south. The Assembly Hall is over 3000 square metres (3600 square yards), containing more than 9700 seats on three tiers, all installed with simultaneous interpretation equipment. Overhead, the vaulted ceiling is illuminated by 500 recessed lights radiating outwards from a gleaming red star. Some 5000 guests can sit down to dinner in the banquet room, which is half the size of a football field. Gilded columns and brilliant lighting combine to produce a sumptuous if overwhelming effect. In addition to the formal public rooms, the Great Hall has 30 separate reception rooms, named after each province, provincial-level city and autonomous region of China (including one for Taiwan).

Chairman Mao's Memorial Hall Standing behind the Monument to the People's Heroes is Chairman Mao's mausoleum. It was built in only one year by teams of volunteers and inaugurated on 9 September 1977, the first anniversary of his death, by his successor to the Communist Party leadership, Chairman Hua Guofeng. This imposing two-tiered edifice resting on a foundation of plum-coloured Huagang stone is supported by 44 granite columns and topped by a flat roof of yellow glazed tiles. It bears a striking resemblance to the Lincoln Memorial in Washington, D.C.

There are three main halls on the ground floor, one to the north, one to the south, and the Hall of Reverence in between. Entering the first, a vast reception area capable of accommodating over 600 people, the visitor will be confronted by a seated statue of Mao carved in white marble. Behind it hangs a painting of Chinese landscape.

Inside the Hall of Reverence, the embalmed body of the late chairman draped with the red flag of the Chinese Communist Party lies in a crystal coffin. The dates '1893–1976' are engraved in gold on a plaque.

Leaving the mausoleum by the south hall, the visitor will see a celebrated poem by the late Mao Zedong inscribed in gold on one of the walls. The walk-through will take less than five minutes, since stopping is not allowed. Security is very strict, and handbags are thoroughly checked at booths outside the entrance before visitors are let in.

The Imperial Palace

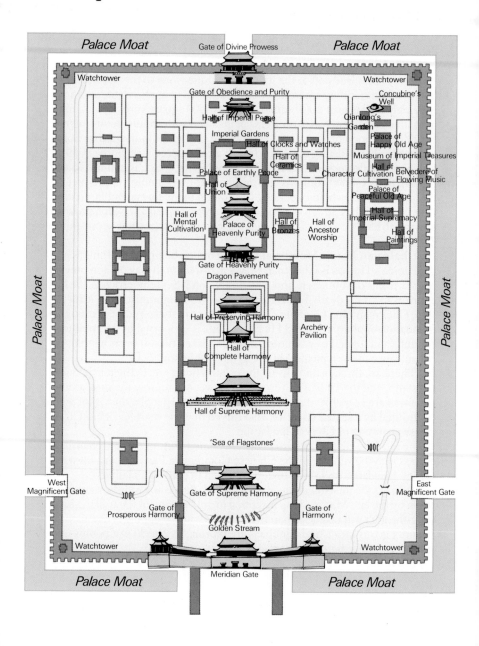

The Imperial Palace (Gugong)

Centre of the Chinese world for nearly 500 years, the Imperial Palace today remains the most complete and best preserved collection of ancient buildings in China. Also called the 'Purple Forbidden City' (Zijincheng) for the exclusive nature of the emperors who built and inhabited it, the Palace is a vast complex of halls, pavilions, courtyards and walls. It is within these walls that 24 emperors of two dynasties, aided by their ministers, eunuch guards, concubines and servants, acted out the drama of ruling imperial China from the early Ming in 1420 to the fall of the Qing in 1911.

Gugong, as it is known to the Chinese, is also a masterpiece of architecture. An extraordinary sense of balance is maintained between the buildings and the open spaces they surround. The scale is monumental but never oppressive; the design symmetrical but not repetitive. True to the Chinese predilection for harmony over diversity, the Palace makes use of a single style of building in an awe-inspiring combination of geomantic planning and aesthetic beauty. All the buildings are carefully laid out on a north-to-south axis, but there is no sense of rigidity to them. Like the Louvre or the Taj Mahal, the Imperial Palace is a monument that can be visited with pleasure again and again.

Originally built in 1420 by over 200,000 workmen at the direction of the third Ming emperor, Yongle, the Palace was nearly burnt to the ground in 1644 during the Manchu takeover. Rebuilt and renovated many times, it nonetheless retains the initial design set down 500 years ago.

The Palace can roughly be divided into three parts. In the foreground are four gates, each of which may look large enough to the first-time visitor to be a palace by itself. Beyond these gates, at the centre of the complex, are three principal halls, of monumental size and scope, where the emperors conducted important State ceremonies. In the rear are three lesser halls, still of notable size, and many smaller courts where the emperors and their families and attendants lived.

With over 9000 rooms spread out over 74 hectares (183 acres), the complex was indeed more like a city than a palace. The visitor entering for the first time may be surprised that each gate and hall leads to yet another, seemingly grander one, at its rear. The effect can be overwhelming and the similarity of design in buildings throughout behoves the visitor to note the special functions of each in order to gain an appreciation for the complexity of the whole. One can, with little imagination, easily understand how the emperors who ruled this Forbidden City could consider themselves at the centre of the universe.

The Palace Gates By passing through the Gate of Heavenly Peace (Tiananmen) and the Upright Gate (Duanmen), one arrives at the imposing Meridian Gate (Wumen), which is the traditional entrance to the Forbidden

City. The horseshoe-shape of the Meridian Gate's massive fortress walls, topped with five towers, seems to draw the visitor submissively forward through the entrance to the inner precincts. This gate was originally used for impressive functions such as reviewing victorious troops and announcing the lunar calendar. Only the emperor himself was permitted to pass through the central opening of the gate, while all others went through the sides.

Beyond this gate lies a courtyard leading to the fourth and final gate, the Gate of Supreme Harmony (Taihemen), a huge open porch supported by red lacquered pillars. One crosses a stream by one of five marble bridges, beautiful pieces in their own right that are dwarfed by the enormity of the surrounding courtyard and palace walls. Note the striking bronze lions guarding this entrance, each with a paw raised to crush a smaller lion, symbolizing the power of the emperor and the subservience demanded by him.

The Principal Halls The next courtyard, called the 'Sea of Flagstones' by the Chinese, was designed to accommodate 90,000 people during an imperial ceremony. In its centre stands the Hall of Supreme Harmony (Taihedian), the largest and grandest structure in the Palace. Here were held the most solemn of ceremonial occasions, such as celebration of the New Year and the emperor's birthday, or announcing the successful candidates of the imperial examinations. This hall is filled with many treasures, including bronze incense burners, musical chimes made of jade, and a nine-dragon screen behind the throne.

Behind the Hall of Supreme Harmony are the Halls of Complete Harmony (Zhonghedian) and Preserving Harmony (Baohedian). In the former, the emperor donned formal regalia before proceeding to the Hall of Supreme Harmony, or performed lesser State functions like inspecting seeds for a new planting. The Hall of Preserving Harmony was used for a time as the site for the highest level of the imperial examinations. Behind this hall, between the descending staircases, is the 'Dragon Pavement', an exquisitely carved block of marble said to weigh over 200 tons.

The Inner Court The three rear halls, the Palace of Heavenly Purity (Qianqinggong), the Hall of Union (Jiaotaidian) and the Palace of Earthly Peace (Kunninggong), were also the site of lesser State functions. During the Ming Dynasty, emperors lived among these buildings, but later, the Qing rulers moved to smaller, less formal parts of the Palace. They nevertheless continued to use the Palace of Earthly Peace to consummate their marriages. The last emperor, Puyi, who ascended the throne as a child and formally abdicated in 1924, was allowed to use this chamber on his wedding night. However, intimidated by the colour scheme of gaudy red (the traditional colour of joy), he fled to his usual quarters.

The east and west sides of the Palace's rear section contain a dizzying succession of smaller courts where the imperial families, concubines and attendants lived, schemed for power and engaged in their many intrigues. In

Palace eunuchs at the Qing Court. These attendants performed a variety of services, and some of the most ambitious ones were able to manoeuvre themselves into positions of great power.

the far northeast corner of the complex, behind the Palace of Peaceful Old Age (Ningshougong), is the famous well down which the Pearl Concubine was cast (see page 90). Several of the eastern palaces have been converted into exhibition halls for the collections of the Palace Museum (see page 124).

Two newly-opened sections in the eastern palaces are worth seeing. One is Qianlong's Garden, built for the retirement of the aging emperor (reigned 1736–95). It is a quiet, secluded rock garden with a central pavilion made of fine wood brought from the forests of Sichuan and Yunnan Provinces. One of three smaller pavilions was specially constructed for elaborate drinking games with strong Chinese liquor, a favourite pastime of the emperor.

The Belvedere of Flowing Music (Changyinge) is a three-storey theatre, the largest in the Palace, and a favourite haunt of the Empress Dowager Cixi. Magnificently carved and painted eaves set off the stage where dramas often depicted Buddhist worthies and Taoist immortals swarming all over the boards, dropping from ceilings and popping out of trap doors. The building opposite, where Cixi watched the dramas, has a rich display of silk costumes, stage properties and scripts used by the imperial troupe. There are also drawings of famous productions at the 60th birthday celebrations of Qianlong and Cixi. The latter affair is said to have continued for 10 consecutive days.

Beyond the rear palaces, by the northern gate of the Palace, are the Imperial Gardens. Landscaped with cypress and pine trees that are now hundreds of years old, this is a perfect spot for a rest or a casual stroll.

The Concubine in the Well

If the walls of the Forbidden City enclosed a dazzling Court presided over by enlightened emperors, they also — down the centuries — hid the innumerable plots, intrigues and betrayals that were played out in the struggles for power. It is said that the Forbidden City is a graveyard of souls; within its tortuous precincts, inexplicable deaths and suspected murders were almost a familiar feature of Court life. There were always, at one time or another, the conflicting interests of pretenders, concubines, eunuchs and ministers to be resolved, especially when questions of succession were involved, or when weak emperors — either because of extreme youth or sheer incompetence — could be manipulated by self-seeking regents and corrupt officials.

The method of exterminating rivals by secret murder was employed with particular frequency, even finesse, by the Manchu Empress Dowager Cixi. This venal and selfish woman, who was supreme ruler of China for nearly half a century (from 1861 to 1908), has been regarded with such horror and fascination that, in the popular mind, the facts of her life have become blurred by legend.

As a young woman, Cixi's entered the palace as a low-ranking concubine to Emperor Xianfeng (reigned 1851–61). On producing a son, she was promoted to Concubine of the First Grade, and skilfully charmed the emperor until she held him in thrall. On the emperor's death, she continued her scheming to eliminate her rivals and eventually achieved such considerable power that she was in a position to have herself and her sister, Empress Ci'an, declared as regents during the minority of Emperor Tongzhi, her five year-old

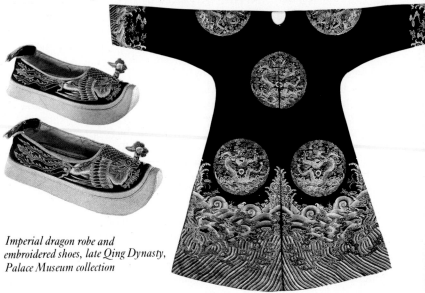

*Imperial dragon robe and
embroidered shoes, late Qing Dynasty,
Palace Museum collection*

son. (Even Ci'an was eventually disposed of, by poison it is said, in 1881). When Tongzhi came of age, Cixi, instead of relinquishing her power, thwarted his attempts to be with his wife and encouraged him in a life of debauchery, which no doubt hastened his death at the age of 18, leaving no heir.

In flagrant defiance of succession laws, Cixi then contrived to put her infant nephew, whom she adopted, on the throne as Emperor Guangxu. She ruled in his name, 'behind a silk screen', until he reached maturity and she ostensibly retired to the Summer Palace in 1889. Nevertheless she continued to meddle in Court affairs. In 1898, in the wake of China's humiliating defeat in the Sino-Japanese War, Guangxu launched the abortive reform movement that was to cost him his freedom. He was kept in semi-captivity by Cixi, who emerged from retirement to assume supreme control of the government once more.

At the height of the chaos following the anti-foreign Boxer Rebellion, the Empress Dowager was to commit one of her most ruthless murders. The date was 15 August 1900. At the time, all of Beijing was in alarm as the Allied troops approached to relieve the besieged legation quarter of foreigners. In the Forbidden City, the Empress Dowager made ready to flee to the western city of Xi'an. Donning the dark blue clothes of a peasant woman, Cixi cut her long lacquered nails and dressed her hair in Chinese style. She summoned the young emperor to prepare by torchlight for their immediate departure in three horse-drawn carts.

At the last moment, the Pearl Concubine (Zhenfei), who was the emperor's favourite, appeared before Cixi and audaciously proposed that either the emperor be allowed to stay in Beijing or that she be allowed to accompany him to the west. Like the Empress Dowager, who had been a concubine herself, this spirited young woman was not given to showing respect or submission to her superiors. She had frequently interfered with Cixi's plans by giving the emperor contrary advice. Now, it must have appeared to the Empress Dowager, the Pearl Concubine had finally over-reached herself.

According to one account, Cixi lost no time in giving orders to her trusted eunuchs, who swiftly wrapped the concubine in a carpet and carried her off, over the young emperor's objections, to the rear of the palace, where they threw her down a well. Her body was recovered a year later and temporarily buried in a field in the city's western suburbs. Later she was laid to rest in the concubines' grave, near Emperor Guangxu's mausoleum, in the Western Qing Tombs.

The well is still there, inconspicuously marked by a small Chinese plaque, in a tiny courtyard in the northeastern corner of the Imperial Palace, by the Palace of Peaceful Old Age. A few Chinese tourists are usually clustered around it, trying to figure out how the eunuchs could have forced someone down so small an opening.

The final mystery surrounding Cixi was the strange coincidence of her death with that of Emperor Guangxu's. It is alleged that Cixi, adamant that the emperor should not outlive her, gave orders from her deathbed for him to be poisoned, but that is just one more sinister intrigue that will never be proved.

Prospect Hill (Jingshan) or Coal Hill (Meishan)

Just north of the Imperial Palace, the site occupied by Prospect Hill was a private park reserved for the use of the emperor in the Yuan Dynasty (1279–1368). During the Ming (1368–1644), an artificial hill with five peaks was made, utilizing earth excavated when the moat of the Imperial Palace was dug. There is an old story that an emperor kept supplies of coal hidden under the hill, hence its other name, Coal Hill (Meishan). A pavilion was erected on each peak, and five bronze Buddhas given pride of place in them. Four of the statues were removed by the troops of the Allied Expeditionary Force when they came to Beijing to relieve the Siege of the Legations in 1900.

Prospect Hill was opened to the public in 1928. Designated as a park after 1949, and closed during the Cultural Revolution, it can now be visited between 6 am and 8 pm.

At the southern approach is the Gorgeous View Tower (Qiwanglou). Previously visited by emperors coming to pay their respects at an altar to Confucius, it is now an exhibition venue for displays of paintings, porcelain and calligraphy.

The best view of Beijing is to be had from the Pavilion of Everlasting Spring (Wanchunting) perched on top of the middle peak, which used to be the highest point in the city. Northwards, one can see the Drum and Bell Towers, a traditional feature of old Chinese cities. To the northwest, the two slabs of water of the Shishahai and Beihai Lake are intersected by Di'anmen Dajie. To the south, the golden roofs of the Imperial Palace can be seen stretching into the distance.

On the eastern slope there used to be an old tree (said to be cassia) from which Chongzhen, the last Ming emperor, is supposed to have hanged himself in 1644. According to one version of the incident, the emperor decamped to the hill upon hearing that rebels intent on overthrowing the dynasty had already stormed the city. He had evidently retreated in some disarray: he wore no head-dress, had only one shoe, and the sleeves of his robe were freshly stained with the blood of his consort and two princesses. The story goes that he committed suicide with his own belt. The spot was once marked by a stone tablet. Later emperors in the early Qing, passing this place to go to the Hall of Imperial Longevity behind the hill, were required to alight from their sedan-chairs and proceed past the tablet on foot, perhaps in order to show more humility when contemplating the salutary example of an unpopular predecessor.

Part of the Hall of Imperial Longevity is now the **Beijing Children's Palace**.

Beihai Park

To the west of Prospect Hill is one of the most beautiful places in Beijing. Beihai Park is open from 6 am to 8 pm (extended to 9 pm in the summer), and is a popular place for skating in the winter and boating in the warmer months. There is a jetty on the northern shore, in front of a botanical garden, from which boats can be easily hired. The extraordinarily beautiful lotus blossoms make late summer a favourite time for visitors.

A lake was first dug here during the Jin Dynasty (12th–13th century); a palace, an island — Qionghua — and pleasure gardens together created a retreat for the Court.

The retreat was refurbished three times during the Yuan Dynasty, and again overhauled in the 15th century by Emperor Yongle, the architect of Beijing. The lake was divided into two: the central lake to the south, Zhong-nanhai, is now reserved for senior members of the Chinese government. Dubbed the 'new Forbidden City' by Beijing residents, **Zhongnanhai** contains the villa where Mao Zedong lived and worked. The complex is off-limits to foreigners but Chinese tours are occasionally admitted. The northern part, Beihai, is open to the public. By the south entrance to the park is the **Round City**, which contains the enormous jade bowl, with fine carvings of sea monsters round the outside, that was given to Kublai Khan in 1265. The Round City is open to visitors from 8:30 am to 4:30 pm.

Qionghua Island The dominant landmark on Qionghua Island is the **White Dagoba**, a Buddhist shrine of Tibetan origin, built in 1651 in honour of the visit of the Dalai Lama to Beijing. Terraces lead down the southern slope, near the bottom of which is the White Dagoba Temple, now known as the **Temple of Everlasting Peace** (Yongansi).

Fangshan Restaurant (see page 43), famous for its imperial dishes, is located among the buildings that form the **Hall of Rippling Waves** (Yilan-tang), a former palace, at the northern end of the island. Not far from this, to the west, is the **Pavilion for Reading Ancient Texts** (Yuegulou), which is a storehouse of 495 stone tablets, engraved with calligraphy during the Qian-long period, including samples of writing from 1500 years ago.

The Northern Shore Over a period of 30 years, Emperor Qianlong embellished several pavilions, halls and terraces along the northwestern shore of the lake. To commemorate his mother's 80th birthday, he had erected the **Ten-thousand Buddha Tower** (Wanfolou) at the western end of the cluster of buildings and gardens. Sadly, the little Buddhas have all been stolen, but the tower is being renovated.

Nearby, in front of the former Temple of Expounding Fortune (Chan-fusi), now the site of a botanical garden, stands the **Iron Screen**, a Yuan-Dynasty wall of volcanic stone carved with strange mythical creatures. A later version, the **Nine-Dragon Screen**, made of glazed tiles in 1417, can be found further east, scaring evil spirits away not from the temple that used to stand behind, but from the Beihai Sports Ground.

Some of the old buildings around Beihai Lake have been converted to modern use; one of the most well-preserved is the **Study of Serenity** (Jingxinzhai) near the northern apex of the lake. This, deservedly called 'a garden within a garden', comprises a quiet walled enclave with a summer house, which now accommodates a literary research institute.

The Empress Dowager Cixi used to go to Beihai for picnics on the lake, and today the park continues to be a favourite with citizens enjoying a snack either from some of the small pavilions serving food, or a full meal at the Fangshan Restaurant.

The Drum and Bell Towers (Gulou and Zhonglou)

Drum and Bell Towers are a traditional feature of an old Chinese city. In Beijing they are located to the north of Prospect Hill.

The Drum Tower (Gulou) dates from the Ming period. Rising from a brick podium, the multi-eaved wooden tower is pierced on two sides by six openings. In imperial times 24 drums would beat out the night watches; now only one of them remains. The tower is being renovated, but it may be entered and climbed.

Not far north of the Drum Tower is the Bell Tower (Zhonglou), a structure 33 metres (108 feet) high. The present tower was constructed of brick in 1747. The copper bell, which replaced an earlier iron bell that is still intact, rang out over the city at seven o'clock every evening until the practice was stopped in 1924.

Song Qingling's House

Song Qingling (Soong Ching-ling), born in 1892 in Shanghai, was married to the famous Republican Sun Yat-sen and became an active political figure in her own right after his death. Though initially aligned, through her husband, with the Nationalist Party (Guomindang), whose leader Chiang Kai-shek married her sister Mei-ling, she eventually split with the right wing and, after spending several year in the Soviet Union, became a supporter of the Communists.

The Chinese accord Song Qingling enormous respect not simply because she was Honorary Chairman of the People's Republic towards the end of her life; she was also, in a very prominent way, a convert from the 'class enemy', coming as she did from a powerful and wealthy Shanghai family.

Her former residence at 46 Beiheyan, near the Back Lake, originally belonged to a member of the Qing royal family. Song Qingling occupied it from 1963 to her death in 1981. It may be visited during 8:30—11:30 am and 1:30—4 pm except on Mondays and Wednesdays, and provides a relaxing diversion from Beijing's major sights. The house is enclosed by a lovely garden filled with pine, cypress and flowering shrubs, as well as traditional pavilions linked by winding corridors. The Fan Pavilion (Shanting) gives a view of the whole garden.

The living quarters have been turned into a modest museum displaying memorabilia of the former occupant's eventful life. Song Qingling was educated at Wesleyan College in Macon, Georgia and the bookshelves contain an impressive collection of English-language books.

Xu Beihong Memorial Museum

This quiet little museum at 53 Xinjiekou Bei Dajie is one of the few public places in Beijing not crowded on a Sunday. It is dedicated to the renowned modern Chinese artist Xu Beihong, who is known internationally for his paintings of horses, and whose style has been widely imitated.

The museum was originally located at Xu Beihong's old home, but that building was demolished to make way for Beijing's subway. The present museum displays Xu's collection of oil paintings, sketches and watercolours simply but effectively. It is an enjoyable place to visit; hours are 9 am – 12 noon, 1 – 5 pm (closed Monday).

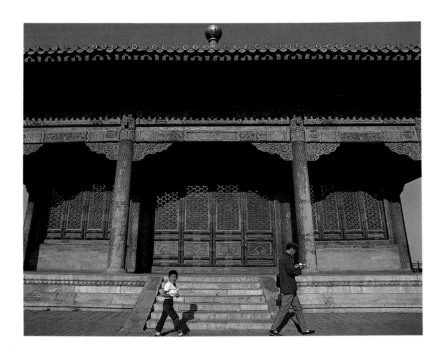

Southern Districts

The Temple of Heaven (Tiantan)

The Temple of Heaven has been called 'the noblest example of religious architecture in the whole of China'. Begun in 1406, in the reign of Emperor Yongle, it was completed in 1420. The huge site — twice the size of the Imperial Palace — is reached by going south along Qianmen Dajie, following a route traversed by past emperors and their entourages in splendid processions from which the commoner had to avert his eyes.

The emperors came to Tiantan at the winter solstice to offer sacrifices to Heaven — momentous occasions for which the temple's grandeur and simplicity provided a fitting background. The temple's design symbolized certain tenets of their beliefs. The altar and temple buildings are located within a wall which is half-circular to the north, and square to the south. During the Yongle period, annual sacrifices to the earth at the summer solstice were also performed here; the outline of the enclosure represented the imagined shapes of heaven (curved) and earth (square). Note that the roof tiles of the Hall of Prayer for Good Harvests (see below) are a deep blue, the colour of the sky. Moreover, each of the main structures in the temple has three tiers, making a total of nine, a number in Chinese cosmology representing Heaven. A separate Altar to the Earth (Ditan) was later constructed to the north of the city.

From the entrance at West Heavenly Gate, an avenue leads to the Hall of Abstinence (Zhaigong). For three days before the rites began, the emperor would have forsworn meat and wine, and the last day of his fast would be spent here. For his safety, the hall was enclosed by a moat.

From there visitors can walk up to the Circular Mound (Yuanqiu), an open altar set on three round marble terraces, built in 1530. The emperor used to come here to commune with Heaven and, interestingly, there is a curious acoustical effect to be heard from the centre of the Circular Mound.

Next to the Mound is the Imperial Vault of Heaven (Huangqiongyu), a wooden structure roofed with blue tiles and built entirely of wood in 1530. Tablets used in ceremonies held on the Mound were stored here. The Imperial Vault is surrounded by a round wall, popularly known as the Echo or Whispering Wall, because of its remarkable acoustics.

Leaving the Imperial Vault, there is a fine walk along a raised approach called the Bridge of Vermilion Stairs to the main building of the park, the magnificent Hall of Prayer for Good Harvests. This round wooden hall is surmounted by a triple roof covered in blue tiles and crowned with a gilded ball. The walls are resplendently painted in rich colours — red, blue, gold and green. It stands on three marble terraces.

The original Hall of Prayer for Good Harvests was built in 1420, but burned down in 1889 and was later reconstructed. This showpiece of

The Temple of Heaven Park

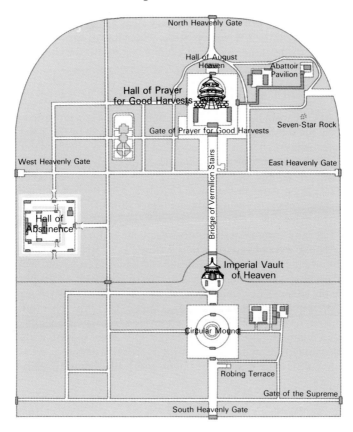

architectural ingenuity, 39 metres (125 feet) high and supported by 28 wooden pillars, stands without the aid of nails.

The Hall was last used in 1914 by Yuan Shikai, then President of the infant Republic, who had imperial ambitions.

Both the Altar and the Hall of Prayer are circular structures enclosed by square courtyards, a design symbolizing the journey from earth to heaven as the supplicant approached the place of worship.

Behind the Hall of Prayer for Good Harvests is the Hall of August Heaven (Huangqiandian), where many of the objects used in the ceremonies are now exhibited.

None of Beijing's other three altars can compare with the Temple of Heaven, but potentially the finest is the **Altar of the Earth** (Ditan), built in

1530, and set in a wooded park in the northeast of the city. The Hall of Abstinence there has already been renovated. Some of the buildings of the **Altar of the Sun** (Ritan), built in 1531, as well as the altar itself, still exist in a pleasant park near the Friendship Store. The **Altar of the Moon** (Yuetan) on the opposite side of the city, also built in 1531, is now the site of a television tower.

The Source of Law Temple (Fayuansi)

Situated in Fayuansi Qian Jie off Niu Jie in the Xuanwumen district, this temple is in the southwest quarter of the city. It was built by the Tang emperor Taizong in AD 654 in memory of troops killed in a battle with the Koreans and has been restored many times since. Two pagodas used to stand beside the temple, but they were destroyed by fire in the middle of the Tang. It was at Fayuansi that the Song Minister Xie Dieshan, brought under guard by Yuan troops to Beijing, chose to starve himself to death rather than submit to the Mongols.

The Fayuansi comprises six courtyards planted with lilac trees. In the past, the temple was obliged to lay on a series of vegetarian banquets every spring for local dignitaries, for it is an age-old Chinese custom to spend a convivial evening wining and dining with crowds of friends on the pretext of admiring the season's new blooms.

The present occupants belong to the Chinese Buddhist Theoretical Institute, and the temple buildings now provide accommodation and class-rooms for a number of novice monks. Some fine statues in bronze and wood, as well as manuscripts and stone engravings, are on display.

The temple is open 8:30 am–12 noon and 1:30–4 pm. It is closed on Wednesdays.

Niu Jie Mosque (Niu Jie Qingzhensi)

Of the 80-odd mosques in Beijing, this one, right in the centre of the city's Moslem district, is the largest and oldest — it was built in AD 996 by Nazruddin, son of an Arab priest. The mosque is open daily from 4 am to 7 pm.

The exterior of the mosque gives very little hint that it is other than a temple, but inside the gate there is a hexagonal Tower for Viewing the Moon, serving an Islamic purpose. This structure enables the imam to determine the beginning and end of Ramadan according to sightings of the moon. Grouped round courtyards behind the tower are the main prayer hall with its entrance facing west (towards Mecca), a stele pavilion, the minaret from which the muezzin calls believers to prayer, a bath-house and some classrooms. The prayer hall is decorated in bright red and gold, with a section reserved for women behind a screen. The ornamentation of the buildings is an blend of Arabic influence and traditional Chinese craftsmanship, a hybrid style which characterizes many mosques in China.

Islam was introduced to China in the Tang Dynasty (618–907) and today the religion is embraced by several racial minorities in the country as well as the Hui, a more widespread community of Moslems distinguishable from the ethnic Chinese only by the faith they profess.

Prospect Garden (Daguanyuan)

In 1986 a new park, complete with pavilions, ponds, miniature hillocks and piped music, was opened to the public. Located in the southwest corner of the city, this pleasure ground has been built in imitation of the garden meticulously described in the great Chinese classic, *The Dream of the Red Chamber* (Honglou Meng) by Cao Xueqin. As recounted in the novel, the name 'Daguanyuan' was chosen by Imperial Concubine Yuanchun on a visitation. She wrote:

> Embracing hills and streams, with skill they wrought
> Their work at last is to perfection brought.
> Earth's fairest prospects all are here installed,
> So 'Prospect Garden' let its name be called!

(From *The Story of the Stone*, translated by David Hawkes)

Although somewhat lacking in authenticity, Daguanyuan is a pleasant park which is already drawing crowds of local visitors.

Western Districts

The Temple of the White Dagoba (Baitasi)

The 48 metre (150 feet)-high Yuan-Dynasty dagoba, off Fuchengmennei Dajie, dominates the city's northwestern skyline. It is to the west of the White Dagoba in Beihai Park.

Even at the time it was completed in 1279, under the supervision of a famous Nepalese architect, it was considered one of the gems of the Mongols' new capital. A large monastery was established here by Kublai Khan which was later destroyed, but rebuilt and renamed Miaoying Temple during the Ming Dynasty. A beautiful filigree copper canopy, hung with bells, tops the dagoba.

The temple suffered damage during the Cultural Revolution and in the 1976 earthquake, but it has now been restored. The four existing halls date from the Qing and contain Yuan and Ming Buddhist statues and Tibetan tankas. During the restoration Buddhist scriptures and other relics dating from the Qianlong period were discovered and are now on display.

White Dagoba, Beihai Park

The Five Pagoda Temple (Wutasi)

In the reign of Ming emperor Yongle (reigned 1403–24) a temple, to be named Zhenjuesi (Temple of the True Awakening), was ordered to be built on this site. It was to house a model of the famous ancient Indian Buddhist temple in Bodhgaya that was presented by an Indian monk to the Court. In 1473, in the reign of Emperor Chenghua, a building with five pagodas, based on the Bodhgaya model, was finally constructed here. Ransacked by English and French troops towards the end of the Qing, the temple never recovered its former glory. The five-pagoda building still stands, however, and its stone bas-relief carvings of figures and flowers, which are beautiful and varied, have been preserved.

The Big Bell Temple (Dazhongsi)

This charming small temple near the Friendship Hotel on the West Ring Road (Beihuan Xi Lu) in the northwest corner of the city was built in 1733. In 1743 a huge bell was brought here, and the temple's name was changed to Dazhongsi. The giant bronze bell is believed to have been cast in the Ming Dynasty, during the reign of Yongle, and is by this reckoning more than 550 years old. Over 7 metres (nearly 23 feet) high and weighing 46 tons, it is inscribed with Buddhist scriptures in Chinese characters and is regarded as one of China's national treasures.

The bell is housed in a tower at the back of the temple, in an inner courtyard. Also displayed in the courtyard are some 30 bronze bells from various periods, showing the high degree of skill and workmanship that had been achieved. One can go right to the top of the Bell Tower by climbing a spiral staircase.

Beijing Zoo (Beijing Dongwuyuan)

The zoo is located in the northwest part of the city. Visitors usually go straight to see the giant pandas to the left of the main entrance, but there are many other interesting animals to be seen — among them tigers from the northeast, yaks from Tibet, enormous sea-turtles from China's seas, and lesser-pandas from Sichuan.

The zoo is open from 7:30 am to 6 pm.

Eastern Districts

The Lama Temple (Yonghegong)

The Lama Temple or the Palace of Harmony and Peace was built in 1694. It can be found on Dongsi Bei Dajie in the northeast of Beijing.

The prince who eventually became Emperor Yongzheng (reigned 1723–35) lived in this palace. Chinese tradition requires an emperor's former residence to be used as a temple upon his accession to the throne, so the palace was duly converted to serve a religious function.

Under the Qianlong Emperor it became a centre of learning for the Yellow Hat sect of Tibetan Lamaism with considerable religious and political sway. As the residence of a 'Living Buddha' it had, at one time, a community of 1500 Tibetan, Mongol and Chinese lamas. Today there are some 70 Mongolian lamas tending the temple.

The complex is arranged as a series of five halls and courtyards leading from a long pretty garden at the entrance. Passing drum and bell towers and two stele pavilions to left and right, the visitor reaches the Hall of the Celestial Guardians (Tianwangdian). Inside is a statue of Maitreya, the Buddha to Come, flanked on four sides by the Celestial Guardians of the East, South, West and North. Also revered is a statue of Wei Tuo, whose meritorious deeds, it is said, included the safeguarding of a bone of Buddha's.

Coming out of Tianwangdian, the visitor will come upon a large copper *ding* (ancient cauldron), cast in 1747. It has been claimed that there are only two examples of this type of *ding* in the whole of China.

The Great Stele Pavilion comes next: it contains a square stele inscribed in four languages (Han, Manchu, Mongolian and Tibetan) describing the philosophy of Lamaism.

The main hall, the Hall of Harmony and Peace, from which the temple takes its name, contains three statues of the Buddha — past, present and future — and at their side figures of the 18 *luohan* (disciples who had vowed always to remain on earth to spread the teachings of Buddha).

To the north of the Hall of Eternal Blessing (Yongyoudian), is the Hall of the Wheel of the Law (Falundian). Its roof supports five small pavilions each surmounted by a little lama pagoda. In the middle of the hall is a statue of Zongkapa (1417–78), a monk who became the mentor of the first Dalai Lama and who founded the Yellow Hat Sect. Against the walls a collection of several hundred Tibetan scriptures is stored.

The last hall, the three-storeyed Pavilion of Ten-thousand Fortunes (Wanfuge) contains a unique example of Chinese carpentry — a massive statue of Maitreya. Standing over 23 metres (75 feet) high, his head reaches the third floor. The statue is supposed to have been carved out of a single white sandalwood tree, transported all the way from Tibet in the mid 18th century.

The low galleries lining both sides of some of the courtyards were originally study halls for the lamas and now contain a fine collection of Tibetan bronzes and *tanka* paintings.

The temple is open from 9 am to 5 pm, and closed on Tuesdays and Thursdays.

The Old Observatory (Guanxiangtai)

Kublai Khan established an observatory at the southeastern corner of his city and it is still there today. Functioning as part of the more modern Beijing Observatory and Planetarium (which is right at the other end of the city, opposite the Beijing Zoo in the northwest), the Old Observatory is now a museum with a small collection of superb Ming and Qing astronomical instruments.

Of the instruments that were made from the 15th century onwards only 15 pieces remain, including several made by Jesuit fathers — notably Adam Schall and Ferdinand Verbiest — in the 17th century. When these missionaries came to China they proved themselves to be such skilful astronomers that they were put in charge of the observatory.

These instruments were taken to Germany in 1900, as spoils of war after the Allied forces had subdued the Boxer Rebellion, but were returned to China in 1919. Eight of them are displayed on the Observatory terrace here, atop one of the few remaining sections of the old city wall (the other seven were moved to the Nanjing Observatory in 1931). They include three armillary spheres, a quadrant, a sextant, a celestial globe, a horizon circle and a quadrant altazimuth.

The observatory may be visited during 9–11:30 am and 1–4:30 pm but is closed on Fridays.

Hutongs

Beijing's *hutongs* — backalleys — are where Chinese life can be seen at its most typical and traditional.

Mostly doomed to be torn down and redeveloped for modern housing blocks, these fascinating little streets form a miniature grid of walled courtyards and passage ways, in between the sweeping boulevards which are the main traffic arteries.

Often blessed with picturesque names — like Little Trumpet Lane and Big Trumpet Lane — the *hutongs* are essentially residential areas where the informality of ordinary life can be witnessed. Pot plants nod at the visitor passing by, and a canary in a cage mocks the rare cat which slinks over an old, grey-plastered wall. Old men dawdle with their long-stemmed pipes, and grandma takes the well-padded baby out for a stroll.

Sometimes a commune donkey-cart loaded with vegetables seeks passage along the narrow lanes, and teenagers loaf around joking. The walls are daubed with slogans such as 'Observe Hygiene' and 'Look After Soldiers' Families Well' but the air of perpetual afternoon overpowers propaganda.

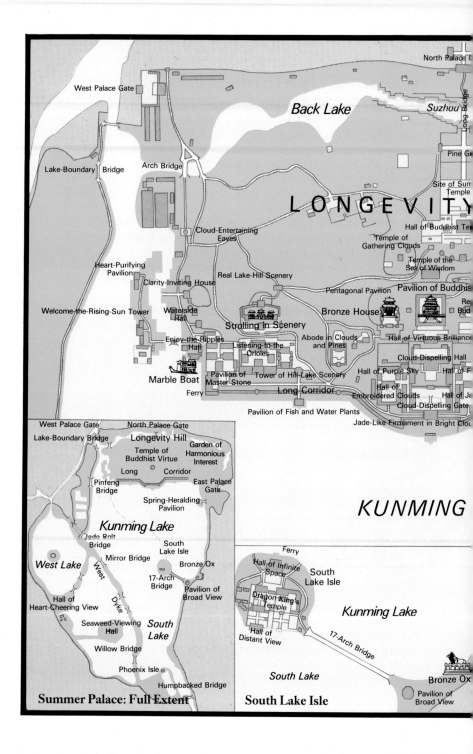

North Palace G

West Palace Gate

Back Lake

Suzhou

Pine G

Lake-Boundary Bridge

Arch Bridge

Site of Sun
Temple

LONGEVITY

Hall of Buddhist Te

Cloud-Entertaining
Eaves

Temple of
Gathering Clouds

Heart-Purifying
Pavilion

Temple of the
Sea of Wisdom

Clarity-Inviting House

Real Lake-Hill Scenery

Pentagonal Pavilion   Pavilion of Buddhis

Welcome-the-Rising-Sun Tower

Waterside
Hall

Bronze House

Re
Bud

Strolling in Scenery

Enjoy-the-Ripples
Hall

Listening-to-the
Orioles

Abode in Clouds
and Pines

Hall of Virtuous Brilliance

Pavilion of
Master Stone

Tower of Hill-Lake Scenery

Hall of Purple Sky

Cloud-Dispelling Hall

Hall of F

Marble Boat

Ferry

Long Corridor

Hall of
Embroidered Clouds

Hall of Ja

Cloud-Dispelling Gate

Pavilion of Fish and Water Plants

Jade-Like Firmament in Bright Clou

West Palace Gate   North Palace Gate

KUNMING

Lake-Boundary Bridge

Longevity Hill

Temple of
Buddhist Virtue

Garden of
Harmonious
Interest

Pinfeng
Bridge

Long   Corridor

East Palace
Gate

Spring-Heralding
Pavilion

Kunming Lake

Jade Bolt
Bridge

Mirror Bridge

South
Lake Isle

West Lake

Ferry

Bronze Ox

Hall of Infinite
Space

South
Lake Isle

17-Arch
Bridge

Pavilion of
Broad View

West

Dyke

Dragon King's
Temple

Kunming Lake

Hall of
Heart-Cheering View

Seaweed-Viewing
Hall

South
Lake

Hall of
Distant View

17-Arch Bridge

Willow Bridge

Phoenix Isle

South Lake

Bronze Ox

Humpbacked Bridge

Summer Palace: Full Extent

South Lake Isle

Pavilion of
Broad View

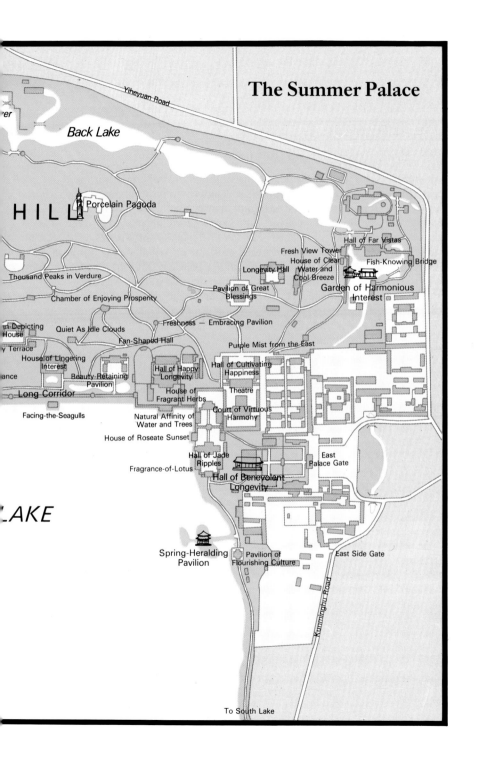

The Summer Palace

Yiheyuan Road

Back Lake

HILL

Porcelain Pagoda

Hall of Far Vistas

Fresh View Tower
House of Clear Water and Cool Breeze

Fish-Knowing Bridge

Longevity Hall

Garden of Harmonious Interest

Thousand Peaks in Verdure

Pavilion of Great Blessings

Chamber of Enjoying Prosperity

Freshness — Embracing Pavilion

Purple Mist from the East

-Depicting House

Quiet As Idle Clouds

Fan-Shaped Hall

y Terrace

House of Lingering Interest

Hall of Cultivating Happiness

ance

Beauty-Retaining Pavilion

Hall of Happy Longevity

House of Fragrant Herbs

Theatre

Long Corridor

Facing-the-Seagulls

Natural Affinity of Water and Trees

Court of Virtuous Harmony

House of Roseate Sunset

Hall of Jade Ripples

Fragrance-of-Lotus

Hall of Benevolent Longevity

East Palace Gate

LAKE

Spring-Heralding Pavilion

Pavilion of Flourishing Culture

East Side Gate

Kunming Road

To South Lake

Sights outside Beijing

The Northwest

The Summer Palace (Yiheyuan)

In order to avoid the intense heat of the summer, the imperial Court used to leave the Forbidden City and stay in a specially-built resort about 11 kilometres (7 miles) northwest of Beijing. Known in the west as the Summer Palace and in China as Yiheyuan — the Garden for Cultivating Harmony — the resort encompasses Longevity Hill (Wanshoushan) and a series of palaces, pavilions, terraces and covered walks strung out along the northern shore of Kunming Lake. Indeed the Summer Palace is three-quarters covered by water and Kunming Lake, whose shape and size have been altered many times by successive landscape architects, is central to the overall design of the park. The indefatigable Emperor Qianlong, for one, reorganised it to resemble the West Lake in Hangzhou in 1751, the year of his mother's 60th birthday (Longevity Hill was named for her).

The Summer Palace and the older Yuanmingyuan (see page 110) were ravaged by Anglo-French troops in 1860. In 1888 the Empress Dowager Cixi diverted funds allocated for improving the navy to the Summer Palace's renovation. She gave it its present name, Yiheyuan, and retired to its peaceful environs in 1889. Following further destruction in 1900, the Summer Palace was again restored at great expense.

The Summer Palace today is a delightful park, informal and less imposing than the Imperial Palace. Much has been restored and it is in a fine state of preservation.

Imperial Residences Directly opposite the East Palace Gate (Donggongmen), across a large courtyard, is the Hall of Benevolent Longevity (Renshoudian) where Cixi and her nephew, the nominal emperor Guangxu, gave audience to their ministers. Behind the courtyard were the private apartments of the imperial household, the Hall of Jade Ripples (Yulantang) This residence was made even more private when the Empress Dowager had a wall erected on its lake side. Here Guangxu was for 10 years her prisoner, having flouted her authority by giving his support to an ill-fated reform movement in 1898. With him safely under guard (but officially 'chronically ill'), she emerged from 'retirement' to assume control of the government once more.

Cixi's own quarters were in the Hall of Happy Longevity (Leshoutang), with Longevity Hill behind and a pleasant lake view in front. Both sets of private apartments, hers and Guangxu's, contain contemporary Qing furniture.

Another part of the compound is the Court of Virtuous Harmony (Deheyuan), made up of the Hall for Cultivating Happiness (Yiledian) and a theatre, built at the cost of 700,000 taels of silver to commemorate Cixi's 60th birthday. She was inordinately fond of theatricals and *tableaux vivants*, and even appeared in them herself. In this theatre a water tank had been sunk under the stage in order to provide such touches of verisimilitude as trickling streams and gushing fountains. The building, now renovated as a theatre museum, should not be missed. Attendants dressed in Qing-Dynasty clothes are on hand to direct visitors to superb exhibitions of theatre costumes and stage props. A collection of Cixi's personal possessions is also on display. These include the automobile — the first imported into China — presented by Yuan Shikai, the military commander who was later President of the new Republic for a brief time; silver and gold ware; brushes, garments and perfumes. The Hall for Cultivating Happiness now displays over 200 historical artifacts, among them the four large carved screens inlaid with jade which are considered national treasures.

Kunming Lake's Northern Shore From the *pailou* (ceremonial arch) on the northern shore of Kunming Lake, the Cloud-Dispelling Hall (Paiyundian), the Hall of Virtuous Brilliance (Dehuidian), the Pavilion of Buddhist Incense (Foxiangge) and the Temple of the Sea of Wisdom (Zhihuihai) rise straight up the slope of Longevity Hill. Inside the Cloud-Dispelling Hall, where Cixi celebrated her birthdays, are displays of *penjing* (potted miniature landscapes) and artifacts which were almost all tributes from her ministers. The oil painting of the empress was executed by an American for Cixi's 69th birthday (see page 108).

The Long Corridor Following the shoreline of the lake, the Long Corridor — 730 metres (795 feet) in length — leads from the Hall of Happy Longevity to the ferry pier beside the Marble Boat. All along it views of the lake mingle with pictures of birds and flowers, scenes from legends and famous landscapes that have been painted on the beams of the roofed walk. The Chinese like to compare the promenade with a picture gallery, and say that so beguiling is the beauty that no courting couple can emerge at the other end unbetrothed.

South Lake Isle From beside the Marble Boat (actually made of stone), below the Summer Palace's popular lunch restaurant Pavilion for Listening to the Orioles (see page 44), it is possible to take a small ferry across the water to the South Lake Isle (Nanhu Dao) and the Dragon King's Temple (Longwangmiao). One of two small villas, now managed by Club Méditerranée (see page 31), is located on the island. From Nanhu you can walk across the Seventeen-Arch Bridge (Shiqikongqiao) back to the entrance.

The Summer Palace is open from 7 am to 7 pm (9 pm in summer). Entrance tickets are sold up to 5:30 pm.

A Portrait of Empress Dowager Cixi

Every year, on her birthday, at an auspicious hour, the Empress Dowager would set free 10,000 caged birds. It must have been a spectacular sight to see her and her entourage in the snow-covered grounds of the Summer Palace as she opened cage after cage of exotic and brilliantly coloured birds and then prayed fervently that they would not be recaptured. By doing this, she hoped that Heaven would be good to her in her next life. She did not realize that her eunuchs were waiting on the other side of the hill to resell as many of the birds as they could catch.

Most of what is known about the Court of imperial China concerns the late 19th and early 20th centuries, for it was only then that eyewitness accounts were written. Before that, Court life was meticulously hidden from the curious eyes of outsiders, whether Chinese or foreign.

It was the Empress Dowager Cixi, effective ruler of China from 1861 to 1908, who began, in her 60s, to invite the ladies of the foreign legations to visit her at Court. Moreover, her chief Lady-in-Waiting was De Ling, daughter of a Manchu official, who had been brought up in France. In De Ling, Cixi found someone who could bridge Chinese and western cultures, and explain to her the many puzzling features of western ways.

In 1903, Mrs Conger, wife of the American Minister to Beijing, persuaded the Empress Dowager to allow her portrait to be painted so that it could be shown at the World Exposition of St Louis. This was a novel idea to the Chinese whose portraits were painted only after death. The American artist Katherine Carl, sister of the Commissioner of Customs in Chefoo, thus became the first foreigner since Marco Polo to stay in the Imperial Palace, and the first foreigner ever to enter the ladies' quarters. The portrait, measuring six foot by four — disappointingly small in Cixi's opinion — is now owned by the U.S. Government and hangs in the Freer Gallery of Art in Washington. Two or three other paintings of the empress were left with her in Beijing.

Miss Carl wrote an account of her unique experience, of her impressions of her surroundings — her surprise at the 85 clocks in the Throne Room, where she painted the portrait — and of the kind and considerate treatment she received from Cixi. But it is only on reading De Ling's recollections that we see how anxious Cixi was that Miss Carl should not become too well acquainted with Court life. De Ling was charged to remain constantly with Miss Carl and specifically commanded not to teach the American any Chinese. Cixi was concerned that Miss Carl should not see the eunuchs punished, lest she should consider the Court officials savages.

Cixi's secretiveness pervaded all her dealings with foreigners. A special Court language was used when in the presence of foreigners who understood Chinese. On one occasion, entertaining some American ladies at the palace, she invited them to see her private sleeping quarters. Unknown to them, however, the previous day had been spent in totally altering the furnishing and fitting of the bedroom so that her real taste and intimate surroundings remained unknown. Chinese subjects were also traditionally forbidden to look at members of the imperial family. Cixi was greatly surprised to learn from Miss Carl that Queen Victoria, whom she very much admired, took walks and carriage rides in public places where she could be seen by the populace at large.

The Empress Dowager was never alone, for even while sleeping she was attended by eunuchs and ladies-in-waiting who were forbidden to fall asleep. She rose early between 5:30 and 6 am. Every morning, with Emperor Guang-xu, her adopted son, she would receive her ministers and generals and deal with matters of State. The rest of the day would be given over to diversions. Both Katherine Carl and De Ling describe walks in the palace grounds, boat trips on the lake and games of dice. There were also theatrical performances of which the empress was particularly fond.

If the day was filled with diversions, the year at the Court was punctuated by festivities. Birthdays, the New Year, weddings, accessions and the seasonal festivals were celebrated with fireworks, day-long performances by eunuchs and Court troupes, presentation of gifts and extravagant banquets at which glittering gold, silver and jade tableware would be heaped with hundreds of delicacies. On these occasions the imperial family and their officials wore their grandest robes and the usual business of the Court was suspended for several days.

Pavilion of Buddhist Incense, Yiheyuan

The Old Summer Palace (Yuanmingyuan)

Not far from the Yiheyuan is the site of the old Qing Summer Palace, Yuanmingyuan. Little is left of it now except some broken pillars and masonry lying about in a field. There is a museum — the Garden History Exhibition Hall — with a well-arranged display of drawings and models

The Garden of Perfection and Brightness

The ruins of the old Qing Summer Palace, Yuanmingyuan, barely conjure up the former glory of the 'Garden of Gardens'. Yuanmingyuan — the garden of Perfection and Brightness — was first established by Emperor Yongzheng (reigned 1723–35), although several gardens had existed on this site since the Ming Dynasty.

From the Ming to the early Qing, garden-making gained enormous popularity and the art of taming disordered landscape and yet preserving its 'naturalness' reached the height of sophistication in the reign of Emperor Qianlong.

The northwestern suburbs of Beijing, stretching right up to the Fragrant Hills, must have appeared eminently suitable for exercising this art. The area is a large plain where terrain and natural springs provided ideal conditions for creating the private gardens and lavish resorts that came to be established there. The Fragrant Hills resort palace was one of these; the Garden of Care-free Spring (Changchunyuan) was another. In due course the whole area became almost totally the exclusive pleasure grounds of emperors and their kinsmen.

Changchunyuan was more than an imperial garden. Emperor Kangxi had a palace built so that he could administer State affairs there as well as in the Forbidden City. To the north of Changchunyuan was Yuanmingyuan, a private garden bestowed on Prince Yinzhen, Kangxi's fourth son, in 1709. On Yinzhen's accession, he embarked on a massive project to extend and transform Yuanmingyuan into a resort fit for an emperor. The Auspicious Sea (Fuhai) was excavated at that time. Water was in fact the dominant theme of the garden and extensively used by landscape artists in designing architectural groupings, scenic spots or formal views. From the time Prince Yinzhen ascended the throne as the Yongzheng Emperor, five successive rulers moved their Court to Yuanmingyuan after each New Year. Except for excursions to Chengde during the summer, they lived in Yuanmingyuan until the winter solstice.

Under Emperor Qianlong Yuanmingyuan became even more splendid. From his inspection tours of the area around the Yangzi River, the emperor assimilatd and then transplanted garden-making ideas and scenery from the south. Altogether 69 'scenes' or 'views' were created in the Summer Palace. Forty of them were recorded by Yongzheng's Court painters Shen Yuan and showing the splendour of the palace in its heyday.

The museum is part of a recent effort to turn the site into a public park, with some shrubs, trees and a few paths for the many citizens of Beijing — who can bicycle here in about half an hour — seeking a respite from their urban surroundings.

Tang Dai, and it is from these scrolls that historians have reconstructed a broader picture of this outstanding garden. Descriptions of it have also survived in the correspondence of the Catholic missionaries employed by the Qing Court. One of them, the Jesuit artist Giuseppe Castiglione, was commissioned by Qianlong in 1745 to design the European-style Western Mansions (Xiyanglou) that were constructed along the northern wall. It is the ruins of these extraordinary palaces that remain today.

In 1860 when Anglo-French troops captured Beijing, rampaging soldiers, on the orders of Lord Elgin, set fire to Yuanmingyuan. A young captain of the British Royal Engineers, who was later to gain fame as 'Chinese Gordon', wrote after the destruction: '[We] went out, and, after pillaging it, burned the whole place, destroying in a Vandal-like manner most valuable property which would not be replaced for four millions. We got upwards of £48 a-piece prize money before we went out here; and although I have not as much as many, I have done well.

'The people are civil, but I think the grandees hate us, as they must after what we did to the Palace. You can scarcely imagine the beauty and magnificence of the places we burnt. It made one's heart sore to burn them; in fact, these palaces were so large, and we were so pressed for time, that we could not plunder them carefully. Quantities of gold ornaments were burnt, considered as brass. It was wretchedly demoralizing work for an army. Everybody was wild for plunder.'

Thirteen years later an attempt was made to rebuild the palace to mark Empress Dowager Cixi's 40th birthday, but dwindling funds put a full-scale restoration out of the question. It was once again devastated in 1900, this time by the Allied Expeditionary Force who relieved the Siege of the Legations. Over the years the damage was compounded by local peasants scavenging for building materials.

In 1977 maintenance of the ruins of Yuanmingyuan was put in the charge of the Beijing municipal authorities, and a small museum has been set up at the site to show the scale and magnificence of the palace in its day. Despite these efforts at conservation, the area remains a wilderness with a few romantic rococo ruins for children to climb on when families picnic there. Energetic Beijing residents say that the best time to visit Yuanmingyuan is at dawn. To many other Chinese it remains a powerful symbol of imperial folly and western aggression.

Hall of Prayer for Good Harvests

The Temple of the Sleeping Buddha (Wofosi)

This temple, 19 kilometres (12 miles) from the city, is reached by continuing west on the road from the Summer Palace towards the Fragrant Hills, passing Jade Spring Hill with its distinctive twin pagodas.

There is mention in the historical records of an enormous statue of the recumbent Buddha first being cast at the temple in the 14th century, but the present statue probably dates from a later period. The Buddha, in lacquered bronze, lying full length with his head supported by his right arm, is five metres (16 feet) long. Enormous shoes which have been presented to the Budddha are displayed in cases on either side. Some rare trees grow in the surrounding countryside, and a line of ancient evergreens leads up to the temple's portico.

The Temple of Azure Clouds (Biyunsi)

A short way from the Temple of the Sleeping Buddha on the road leading to the Fragrant Hills is one of Beijing's great temples, the Temple of Azure Clouds. A temple has stood here since the Yuan Dynasty. It was restored and extended on two separate occasions by palace eunuchs Yu Jing and Wei Zhongxian, who planned to place their graves in the hill behind (they both failed in their ambition). There are many buildings here, arranged on the side of a hill, and much to see. At the top of the hill is the Diamond Throne Pagoda, an Indian-style stone temple with a spectacular view from its roof. It was built on the lines of the Five Pagoda Temple (see page 101) in 1792. Below is the Memorial Hall to Sun Yat-sen. After his death in 1925 the body of the founder of modern China lay in state in this temple, reposing in a crystal coffin presented by the Soviet Union. His body was moved to Nanjing in 1929 when the mausoleum there had been completed.

To one side of the Memorial Hall is the Luohan Hall, with its four inner courtyards, which was built in the mid 18th century. *Luohan* are the disciples of Buddha, and over 500 gilded wooden statues of these proselytes, each one quite distinct with an individual, and very human, personality, are crammed into this section of the temple complex.

Biyunsi, open between 8 am and 5 pm, makes for a particularly delightful excursion in the spring, when the peach and almond trees — both within the temple complex and on the surrounding hillsides — are covered in blossom.

Fragrant Hills Park (Xiangshan Gongyuan)

Close to the Temple of Azure Clouds, this park is set in a belt of hills northwest of Beijing, about 40 minutes' drive away. The Western Hills, as the area is also called, has long been a favourite retreat of the emperors. In the 12th century when it was a royal hunting park, the landscape was considered so picturesque that the hills came to be designated as one of the Eight Great Scenes of Yanjing (the City of Swallows). With the addition of a resort palace in the reign of Kangxi, its attractions further increased until the park reached the peak of its splendour in the 18th century.

Roads fan out from the main east-facing gate. To the left is the Fragrant Hills Hotel (see page 31), a recent construction. Many of the old beauty spots still remain, however, most notably at the northern end of the park. One can reach this part by entering through the north gate from the direction of the Temple of Azure Clouds. Crossing Glass Lake (Yanjinghu) one comes to the Study of Self-knowledge (Jianxinzhai), a 16th-century garden with a circular pool, enclosed by a rounded wall and promenade and shielded by clumps of trees on three sides. To the south of it are the remains of Zhaomiao, a Tibetan-style temple erected in the Qianlong period, as well as an ornamental archway and a pagoda roofed in yellow glazed tiles, with bells dangling from its eaves.

The name 'Fragrant Hills' probably derives from the two slabs of stone — shaped like incense burners — on top of the highest peak at the western extremity of the park. The wisps of mist clinging to the summit resemble, it is claimed, puffs of scented smoke coming from the incense burners at the top. But the park is famous above all for its autumn aspect. The blaze of red on the hillsides when the leaves of the Huanglu smoke tree (sometimes referred to as maple) are turning is a sight that has been celebrated in poetry and painting.

The North

The Great Wall (Changcheng)

The Great Wall, said to be the only man-made structure visible from the moon, has captured the imagination of countless people throughout its long history.

The wall was built in a piecemeal fashion over a long period, from the fifth century BC down to the 16th century AD, as a means of defence against raids from northern nomadic tribes. When the empire was unified under Qin Shi Huangdi in 221 BC, a continuous line of fortifications was ordered to be constructed by joining up the old walls.

'A wall between is a mountain' goes an old saying, and in the hearts of the Chinese, the 'Wall of Ten-thousand Li' (Wanli Changcheng) not only protected them from the barbaric Huns (Xiongnu), its significance lay also in separating the familiar, safe, patterns of settled agriculture, from the alien pastoral nomadic life of the steppes and deserts beyond.

Historical texts record as many as 300,000 men working for 10 years on the construction of a section of the wall. Stories of the hardship suffered by these conscripted labourers, toiling and often dying in the cold mountains, have been passed down, contributing to the image of the Qin emperor as a hated tyrant. Built partly of earth faced with brick and partly of masonry, the Great Wall stretched for 4000 kilometres (2500 miles) from deep in Central Asia to the Bo Gulf of the Yellow Sea. It was lined with ramparts and punctuated by watchtowers, from which smoke signals were sent to the capital at Xi'an by sentries posted at the wall's strategic points.

The Great Wall has fallen into disrepair and then been rebuilt many times through the centuries. In recent years three parts of the wall have been restored. Visitors to Beijing usually go to the section at **Badaling**, in Nankou Pass, about 80 kilometres (50 miles) from the city, either before or after a visit to the Ming Tombs. There is a special train service from Beijing to Badaling, which runs daily in the summer and several times a week off-season. The train goes from Xizhimen station in northwest Beijing (not the main railway station) and tickets can be bought on board. It is also possible to travel up to the wall by taxi or coach, as long as the road is not blocked by snow. CITS and the major hotels organize their own tours. The drive takes around two hours. Helicopter trips over the Great Wall can be arranged at the Holiday Inn Lido (tel. 5006688).

It is extremely cold on the wall in winter, but it is also at its most impressive at this time, when the mountains are covered with snow. In any season, the ideal time to go would be after 3 pm (when all the crowds have left) by arranging one's own transport (Rmb140 by taxi).

The restored section at Badaling dates from the Ming. From the carpark it is possible to climb up onto the wall, and walk either to the left or right.

Both directons are very steep but the awe-inspiring views of the wall snaking off across the mountains make the climb worthwhile.

A newly opened section of the Great Wall is located at **Mutianyu**, northeast of Beijing and also about two hours' drive away. Unlike Badaling, this section is not set in steep and dramatic hills and has quite a different, more peaceful, atmosphere. To get to the wall one has to mount some thousand steps or ride the funicular that has been recently installed.

Chengde: Imperial Resort

Chengde lies 354 kilometres (220 miles) northeast of Beijing and is the site of Jehol, or 'Warm River', the beautiful 18th-century resort of the Manchu emperors of the Qing Dynasty. From 1681 the emperors used to escape the scorching Beijing summer and travel north, over the Great Wall, to the cool hunting grounds of Jehol.

The journey, which took the imperial household at least two weeks, takes today's tourists, travelling by train from Beijing, a mere five and a half hours.

The wooded river basin in which Chengde lies is surrounded by pleated hills, punctuated at intervals by strange rock formations. Emperor Kangxi created the palace, lakes and parks to blend in with the natural beauty of the site. The palace itself is an appropriately simple building, constructed of *nanmu*, a hard aromatic wood. The audience chamber, the Modest and Responsible Hall, is connected to the other chambers by *lang*, or covered walkways, that wind around the courtyards which are themselves shaded by ancient pines.

Through the palace it is only a few minutes' walk to the park and lakes. Emperor Kangxi decreed that 36 beauty spots were to be created in the park. His grandson Qianlong then doubled the number. As you wander beside the lake, there are carefully placed brightly coloured bridges which are designed to arouse your curiosity and lure you to one of the beauty spots — a pavilion such as the Hall of Mists and Rain, or the Golden Hill Pavilion.

Outside the palace grounds, Emperor Qianlong built eight magnificent temples, seven of which still remain. The eighth, which was built of bronze, was removed by the Japanese during the war. The first to be built was the Temple of Universal Peace (Puningsi), in 1775. This was a period in Chinese history of massive annexations, including Tibet and what is now Xinjiang. To integrate and, in some cases, to placate his new subjects, the emperor modelled the temples on their religion and culture. For this reason the Putuozongshengmiao is a copy of the Potala at Lhasa in Tibet.

Jehol lost favour with the Qing Court after the unfortunate — and ominous — accident to Emperor Jiaqing, who was struck dead by lightning there. The summer palace and temples now form part of a public park.

The Ming Tombs (Ming Shisanling)

The valley of the Ming Tombs lies about 48 kilometres (30 miles) north of Beijing. Thirteen of the 16 Ming emperors are interred here, hence the site's Chinese name, Ming Shisanling (The Thirteen Ming Tombs). The tombs were located in accordance with Chinese geomantic specifications requiring graves to be protected by high ground.

The approach is impressive. The modern road passes by a stone portico with five carved archways. This is the beginning of the imposing route known as the Spirit (or Sacred) Way. Next comes the Great Vermilion Gateway; of its three openings the central entrance was reserved for the coffins of deceased emperors, and all followers were required to dismount at this point. The whole tomb site, to which this gateway was the actual entrance, was of course surrounded by a wall, now gone.

The Spirit Way The emperor's coffin would have been borne past a stele pavilion, a typical imperial structure with the floating clouds motif repeated on its supporting columns. The procession of mourners would then have filed along the Spirit Way, a funereal guard of honour of six pairs of animals and six pairs of human figures carved from large blocks of stone. The latter, all standing, are statues of scholars, administrators and warriors. The animals — lions, *xiechi* (a mythical beast), camels, elephants, unicorns, horses — are either standing or crouching. The Spirit Way ends at the Dragon and Phoenix Gate.

In its entirety, this part of the Ming Tombs dates from the 15th century. Beside the road there is now a mass of shrubs and fruit trees. Once across an arched bridge, visitors can then visit the different tombs, scattered round the valley.

Changling The most important tomb, appropriately, belongs to the great Yongle, the third Ming emperor who was responsible for building so much of Beijing. He chose this site and had his burial place built on the traditional plan of a walled enclave, enclosing buildings separated by three courtyards, with the tumulus at its head. The tumulus, marked by a stele tower and traditionally referred to as the Precious Fortress (Baocheng), has not been excavated, but visitors may see inside the magnificent Hall of Sacrifice. This very fine structure built in 1427 is supported by 32 massive wooden pillars wrought from huge trunks of *nanmu* wood from the extreme southwest of China. The Yongle Emperor was interred in the Changling in 1424. Sixteen royal concubines were buried alive in ancillary graves following a custom that was finally discontinued during the reign of the sixth Ming emperor.

Dingling The tomb of the Wanli Emperor (reigned 1573–1620) and his two consorts is known as the Dingling. Its construction was started in 1584, when Wanli was 22, and took six years to complete. It was excavated in

1958, and one may now descend by a modern spiral staircase to the underground tomb behind a stele tower. The vaulted marble palace, built deep underground so that it is cool in summer and comfortably warm in winter, consists of three burial chambers. At the entrance to the antechamber is a carved marble gateway. The floor is paved with specially-made 'golden bricks' which had been fired for 130 days and dipped in tung oil before being laid. The middle chamber contains three marble thrones; in front of each of them are five drumshaped stools for holding offerings and a large glazed pot known as the Ever Bright Lamp. The lamps would have been filled with oil and lit before the tomb was sealed. The back chamber was the actual repository of the royal coffins. On being opened by the excavation team they were found to be stuffed with some 300 assorted garments. Even more lavish, countless pieces of jewellery, curios and porcelain — stowed in 26 lacquer chests — were also deposited to provide for a luxurious life in the nether world. The regalia and the treasure have all been moved to two small exhibition halls outside. They should not be missed.

Another modern addition to the valley of the Ming Tombs has recently been opened — it is a golf course laid out by Japanese investors (see page 57).

The East

The Eastern Qing Tombs (Dongling)

The site of the Eastern Qing Tombs is over the provincial border, in Hebei, some 121 kilometres (75 miles) east of Beijing (a journey of about four hours by car).

The 15 tombs are spread over an area 34 kilometres (21 miles) wide, and built under the lee of Mount Changrui. The choice of this site as the Qing imperial burial ground is attributed to the Shunzhi Emperor, who came upon it when out hunting. He is interred here, together with the Kangxi, Qianlong, Xianfeng and Tongzhi Emperors. Other tombs include those of the Empress Dowager Cixi, several less notorious empresses, concubines and royal children, as well as that of Emperor Kangxi's revered teacher.

There are some striking differences between the Ming and Qing tombs. Whereas the Ming created a single 'Spirit Way' (the approach to imperial burial grounds lined with stone animals and officials), the Qing have several shorter ones leading to tumuli which are also on a smaller scale. The Qing stone figures have their hair in the traditional Manchu plait, and while the scholar is shown wearing a string of beads of Buddhist origin, emblematic of the strong lamaistic leanings of the Manchu rulers, the Ming statues are generally depicted carrying Confucian tablets. The animals too differ in style and decoration.

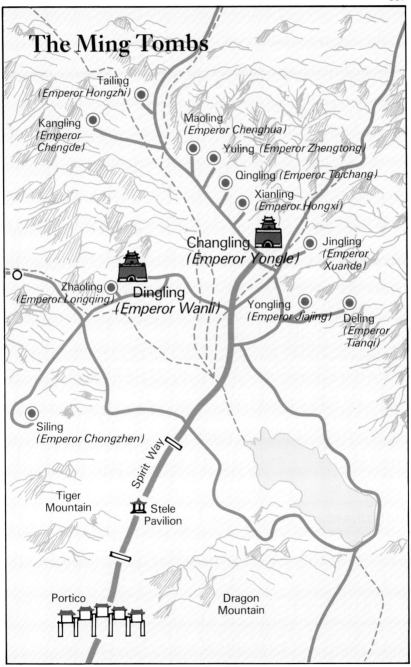

The Ming Tombs

Tailing *(Emperor Hongzhi)*

Kangling *(Emperor Chengde)*

Maoling *(Emperor Chenghua)*

Yuling *(Emperor Zhengtong)*

Qingling *(Emperor Taichang)*

Xianling *(Emperor Hongxi)*

Changling *(Emperor Yongle)*

Jingling *(Emperor Xuande)*

Zhaoling *(Emperor Longqing)*

Dingling *(Emperor Wanli)*

Yongling *(Emperor Jiajing)*

Deling *(Emperor Tianqi)*

Siling *(Emperor Chongzhen)*

Spirit Way

Tiger Mountain

Stele Pavilion

Portico

Dragon Mountain

The tombs of the Qianlong Emperor, the Empress Ci'an and the Empress Dowager Cixi are open to the public. The underground marble vault of Qianlong is particularly impressive: every interior wall and arch is richly carved with images of the Buddha, the Celestial Guardians and with thousands of words of Buddhist scriptures in both Sanskrit and Tibetan. Ornate carving also embellishes Cixi's mausoleum, where one can see the repeated use of such imperial motifs as dragons, phoenixes and clouds. Built over a period of 30 years, the tomb was a subject of great interest to the Empress Dowager, who visited the site several times. Unfortunately both this tomb and that of the Qianlong Emperor were broken into by grave robbers in the 1920s, and the fabulous treasures, buried with the view of ensuring a comfortable afterlife, have all disappeared.

Visitors may like to round off their excursion to the Dongling by calling in at the two small museums that have been established in the sacrificial halls at the tombs of the two empresses, Cixi and Ci'an. Opening times are from 9 am to 4 pm.

The Southwest

Marco Polo Bridge (Lugouqiao)

Proceeding southwest from Guang'anmenwai for about 16 kilometres (10 miles), one reaches the Lugouqiao, celebrated not only for being Beijing's oldest surviving bridge, but also for the impression it made on Marco Polo, who saw it in 1290 (hence the bridge's western name). He has left us with a fine description.

Marco Polo Bridge spans the Yongding River. As early as the Warring States period (475–221 BC), the site of the present bridge had been a strategically important river crossing. Initially the crossing was probably made by a wooden bridge or by pontoons. From the Jin Dynasty onwards, when the capital was at Beijing, increased traffic across the river warranted a more permanent bridge, which was completed in 1192. Constructed with careful reference to the river's flow, this solid stone structure resting on 11 arches has withstood weathering for several centuries. The piers supporting the bridge are especially strong, being reinforced by triangular metal posts which locals used to call 'Swords for Decapitating Dragons' in the belief that evil dragons, seeing these posts, would quietly go away rather than cause mischief for river craft.

On either side of the bridge there is a parapet with 140 columns carved and surmounted with lions. Imperial steles stand at each end; one commemorates the renovation of the bridge in 1698, the other carries a four-character inscription by Emperor Qianlong, 'Bright Moon on Lugou'.

Peking Man Site

The village of Zhoukoudian, which can be reached by train from Beijing, used to be notable for its production of lime. In 1929 it achieved worldwide fame with the discovery of the first skulls of Peking Man. The fossil remains of *Homo erectus pekinensis* have been dated to about 300,000–500,000 years ago.

The limestone caves of Zhoukoudian probably account for the location of a paleolithic settlement here. So far bones of over 40 inhabitants have been unearthed and, with the evidence of other remains, scientists have pieced together a fascinating picture of this early community.

Some of the limestone caves, on the northern slope of Dragon Bones Hill (Longgushan) to the east of Zhoukoudian station, may be visited. There is also a comprehensive museum on the evolution of man and the Zhoukoudian culture. Included in the displays are stone implements used by Peking Man and Upper Cave Man (who lived about 50,000 years ago), fossils of animals hunted by them, and evidence that Peking Man used fire. The whereabouts of the original Peking Man fossils, lost during the Second World War while en route to the United States for safekeeping, is still however shrouded in mystery.

Zhoukoudian is 48 kilometres (30 miles) to the southwest of Beijing. It is best to go with a tour guide as very little information is available in English at the site.

The West

The Temple of the Pool and Wild Mulberry (Tanzhesi)

Situated in the Western Hills, this Buddhist temple lies 45 kilometres (28 miles) west of Beijing. It is reached by a winding road which passes the Ordination Terrace Temple (see below) and some quite spectacular scenery, especially in the spring when the fruit trees are in blossom. One of the biggest and oldest temples in the Beijing area, Tanzhesi has been completely restored in recent years.

A temple known by various names has existed on this site for 1600 years. Its present name is derived from the Dragon Pool nearby and from the trees, growing on the hillside, whose leaves were used to feed silkworms. The present structure, laid out on traditional lines, is typical of Ming and Qing architecture. A ceremonial arch (*pailou*) frames the entrance to a compound of several halls, pavilions and courtyards: there is the Hall of Abstinence, the Ordination Altar and, at the back of it, the Hall to Guanyin, the Goddess of Mercy. The latter is associated with Kublai Khan's daughter, Princess Miaoyan, who entered the nunnery here in the 13th century. Her devotions were performed so assiduously, it is said, that she wore away the piece of stone on which she stood, and left deep footprints on it.

Some of the strangely shaped trees within the temple are said to be a thousand years old.

To the right of the Hall of Abstinence is the Flowing Cup Pavilion (Liubeiting), where dragon-shaped channels feed spring water into the Dragon Pool. This water has a special quality which enables objects to float upon the surface easily. On the third day of the third month people used to gather for the 'purification of the fermented wine'; brimming wine cups were floated down the stream and only when they stopped moving was the wine drunk.

Below the temple are beautiful stone stupas built over the burial sites of the temple's monks dating from the Jin, Yuan, Ming and Qing Dynasties.

The Ordination Terrace Temple (Jietaisi)

The Ordination Terrace Temple (Jietaisi) lies in the Western Hills, 33 Kilometres (22 miles) from Beijing on the road that leads to the Temple of the Pool and Wild Mulberry. There has been a temple in this mountain cleft for 1350 years, but it was in the Liao Dynasty (916−1125) that its chief function — the ordination of Buddhist novices — was established when a monk, Fajun, founded an altar here.

The Ordination Altar, in the northeast courtyard, is of white marble and its three tiers are carved with hundreds of figures, some as tall as a metre (just under three feet). Once a year, at midnight, an initiation ceremony was conducted; the novices, having fasted all day, would endure burns from lighted incense sticks upon their tonsured heads.

As the temple was one of his favoured rest-stops, the Qing emperor Qianlong handsomely endowed it during his reign, and the present buildings date from this period of building and renovation. The ancient pine trees contribute to the temple's peculiar charm. One of them, which sadly no longer survives, is marked with a stone tablet which can be seen to the left of the Thousand Buddha Pavilion behind the temple's main hall. In the time of Qianlong this remarkable pine was dubbed the 'Mobile Tree' on account of its ability to shake all over when any one of its branches was pulled.

Museums

Palace Museum

Although the Imperial Palace in its entirety is regarded as a museum of architectural and artistic heritage, there are specific halls and pavilions within it — collectively known as the Palace Museum — which are used as showcases for the cornucopia of treasures in the palace. As the restoration of the Palace is constantly in progress, new areas of exhibits are opened from time to time.

Visiting hours are 8:30 am–4:50 pm with the ticket offices closing at 3:30 pm. However, the Museum of Imperial Treasures closes at 4:15 pm with the ticket office closing at 3:15 pm.

The Historical Art Museum

Housed in the Hall of Preserving Harmony (Baohedian), the collection here provides a broad conspectus of Chinese cultural development. Arranged chronologically, the exhibition is in three parts. The first part deals with the period from earliest times to about 4000 years ago, illustrated by excavated ancient painted pottery, bronzes and sculptures. The fifth to the 13th centuries — the period covered by the second section — saw the emergence of an early modern style of painting as well as major developments in the art of ivory carving, lacquerware, weaving and calligraphy. The third part of the exhibition shows samples of the arts during the Yuan, Ming and Qing Dynasties; of particular interest is the fine porcelain that was produced in this era.

Serveral special exhibitions of imperial treasures are housed in the Six Eastern Palaces at the rear of the complex.

The Hall of Bronzes

This collection is shown in the Palace of Abstinence (Zhaigong), the Hall of Sincere Solemnity (Chengsudian) and the Palace of Revered Benevolence (Jingrengong), and includes examples of bronze wine goblets, tripod cooking vessels and pots from the Shang, Zhou, Spring and Autumn and Warring States periods.

The Hall of Ceramics

The Palace of Heavenly Favours (Chengqiangong) and the Palace of Eternal Harmony (Yonghegong) contains Neolithic pottery from the Shang to the Western Zhou Dynasties, with examples of Longshan blackware, incised and glazed pottery from the Han Dynasty on through to the celadon ware of the Yuan, the tri-coloured glazes of the Tang and the blue and white of the Ming and Qing Dynasties. Many fine examples from the famous imperial kilns of Jingdezhen can be seen.

The Hall of Paintings
Scroll paintings and calligraphy are displayed in the Hall of Imperial Supremacy (Huangjidian), the Palace of Peaceful Old Age (Ningshougong) and galleries on its eastern, western and southern sides. For a few weeks each autumn, during the dry weather, the rarest examples of Chinese visual arts are brought out for public view.

The Museum of Imperial Treasures
This superb hoard of ritual and everyday items used by the Qing Court is displayed in the Hall of Character Cultivation (Yangxindian) and the Palace of Happy Old Age (Leshougong). The treasures grouped together in the first hall include silver and gold tableware, jewelled knick-knacks and little Buddhist shrines. The latter, generally made of gold, include one made for Emperor Qianlong to preserve a strand of his mother's hair.

In the second hall, which contains the gorgeous habiliments and attire worn by emperors, empresses and concubines, there are exquisite pieces of jewellery, hairpins and head-dresses as well as Court costumes. One of the most outstanding exhibits is Qianlong's peacock feather-trimmed robe studded with seed pearls and tiny coral beads.

The sybaritic Court amassed a vast number of ornaments and decorative pieces to adorn the palace interior. One kind of curio (which is still popular with collectors today) is the jewelled *penjing* — artificial miniature potted landscapes composed of precious stones, with leaves and petals carved out of gold, silver and jade — which are shown in the third section.

Note that although the Museum of Imperial Treasures is open 8:30 am–4:30 pm daily, the ticket office closes at 3:15 pm.

The Hall of Clocks and Watches
A small gallery northeast of the Palace of Earthly Peace (Kunninggong) houses an extraordinary collection of elaborate clocks, both European and Chinese, dating from the 18th and 19th centuries.

Exhibition of Historical Relics from the Qing
Several aspects of imperial life and duties are represented by the relics here in the Palace of Heavenly Purity (Qianqinggong), for example the imperial seals for giving the stamp of royal approval to decrees issued in the emperor's name. There are also musical instruments, more ceremonial and travelling regalia and weapons and arms.

Museum of the Chinese Revolution and Museum of Chinese History

The large building which houses these two museums stands opposite the Great Hall of the People, on the eastern side of Tiananmen Square. It is open 8:30 am–5 pm (admission till 3 pm only) and is closed on Mondays.

Museum of the Chinese Revolution

This occupies the north (left) wing of the building. More than 3300 exhibits, displayed on two floors, illustrate the history of the Chinese Communist Party. The collection of models, documents and materials begin with the May Fourth Movement of 1919 and moves on to the founding of the Party itself, the First Revolutionary Civil War (1924—27), the Second Revolutionary War (1927—37), the Anti-Japanese War of Resistance (1937—45) and the Third Civil War (1945—49). The photographic accounts of this tumultuous period are of particular interest.

Museum of Chinese History

Occuping two floors of the south (right) wing, this permanent exhibition, though badly lit and with Chinese-language captions only, is a most extensive survey of the evolution of Chinese history and culture. Many of the 10,000 items are replicas or copies of objects belonging to provincial museums around the country which are included as an aid to wider understanding. It is chronologically divided into four sections.

The Primitive Society section exhibits fossils from the Paleolithic, Mesolithic and Neolithic eras. Pottery and bronzes illustrate the Shang and Zhou Dynasties. From the Warring States period on through to the early Qing Dynasty, models, samples of fabrics, jewellery, lacquerware, porcelain and weaponry have been assembled to show China's scientific and cultural development. The last section covers the period 1840—1919, with exhibits of cannon, weapons, clothing, flags and manuscripts.

Lu Xun Museum

This museum in Fuchengmennei Dajie commemorates China's outstanding writer of the 20th century, Lu Xun (1881—1936), who is also noted for his considerable contribution to the liberal movement in China in the 1920s.

The museum, which abuts Lu Xun's former Beijing residence, displays manuscripts, letters, and pages from his personal diary. Some 13,000 books from his library are also in the keeping of the museum, as well as items of clothing and other memorabilia. The museum is open 8:30—11 am and 1:30—4 pm. It is closed on Mondays.

Military Museum of the Chinese People's Revolution

This is a permanent exhibition of 5000 items — photographs, directives, military uniforms, weaponry and Eighth Route Army insignias, along with portraits of revolutionary heroes and martyrs — covering the Chinese revolutionary army's 28-year history between 1921 and 1949.

The museum is at 9 Fuxing Dajie. Visitors are asked to present their passport for inspection at the entrance. The museum is open 8:30 am—5 pm and closed on Mondays.

Museum of Natural History

The museum contains four halls devoted to Botany, Zoology, Paleozoology and Paleoanthropology, the latter science being one in which China has contributed much in recent discoveries and research. It is open 8:30 am – 5 pm (admission till 4 pm only), and closed on Mondays.

The Temple of Confucius (Kong Miao) and the former Imperial College (Guozijian)

Situated in Beijing's northeast quarter, close by the Lama Temple, the temple dedicated to Confucius was raised in the Yuan Dynasty and housed the ancestral tablets of Confucius and four other sages. Ceremonials and sacrifices were conducted by the prominent scholars of the day and members of the imperial Court three times a year, including Confucius' birthday.

Part of the temple has been given over to the **Capital Museum**, which exhibits archaeological finds from Beijing and its environs and may be visited between 9 am and 5 pm except on Mondays.

Connected to the museum by a side door is the former **Imperial College**, first built in 1287 and substantially extended in 1784. The focal point of the former college is the square pavilion, which can be thrown open on all four sides by means of doors and shutters, called the Imperial Schoolroom. It is sited in the middle of a pool and reached by bridges. Here the emperor used to lecture on the Classics to ministers and students. On either side of the structure there used to stand 190 stone tablets engraved with 800,000 words of the Thirteen Classics, which took the calligrapher 12 years to transcribe. The tablets have been moved to a courtyard east of the main gate, Taixuemen, and the Imperial College is now the **Capital Library**.

Exhibitions are held from time to time at:
National Gallery of Art (Meishuguan)
Wusi Dajie (at the top of Wangfujing)
Nationalities Cultural Palace (Minzu Wenhua Gong)
Fuxingmennei Dajie

Imperial Examinations

Northeast of the junction of Jianguomen and the highway, in the vicinity of the present Chinese Social Science Institute, is the site of the Ming and Qing Examination Hall (Gongyuan). Nothing is left of it now; its existence is recalled only by the streets — Gongyuan Dong Jie and Gongyuan Xi Jie — and a few hutongs named after it.

The system of imperial examinations, by which candidates were recruited into the ranks of the civil service, had its origins in the Han Dynasty (206 BC–AD 220). As the government of a united and increasingly less feudal China grew more complex, an established, non-hereditary, corps of officials and administrators gradually became the accepted basis of organization.

The competitive examinations tested competence in a broad range of subjects — economics, philosophy, administration — but by the Ming these had narrowed to a highly formalized syllabus based on interpretations of the Confucian classics. The increasingly orthodox responses demanded by examiners culminated in the very stylized 'eight-legged essay' (ba gu wen), a rigid literary form later critics condemned for its tendency to inhibit originality and creative writing.

During the Ming and Qing, examinations were held not only in the capital but also in provincial centres during the autumn. By March, thousands of hopeful candidates would be assembling for the triennial examination in Beijing. For nine days they would be confined in row upon row of tiny cells, being fed meagre meals brought in from outside and closely guarded by invigilators, to scribble away at their 'eight-legged essays' in the hopes of dazzling rewards. Success meant being received by the emperor in one of the sumptuous halls of the Imperial Palace and the privilege of joining the ruling elite. Indeed, by 1400, the examination was the only guaranteed means of entry into the imperial service. While the system was not immune to corruption — invigilators were bribed, cribs were smuggled in — it did furnish scores of talented sons of peasant families with brilliant careers and political advancement.

The ideal of the loyal scholar-official has remained a figure of awe to the Chinese to this day. Stories of their erudition and civilizing influence on warrior-emperors abound. They tell of dutiful ministers who expounded the moral precepts and historical precedents set down by ancient sages, and related them to the political issues of the day. By gentle reminders that an emperor's mandate to rule depended on 'government by righteousness', they curbed the worst excesses of their arrogant sovereigns.

This system of competitive entry to the civil service came to be adopted by countries outside of China but, by the late 19th century, profound scholarship was no longer an adequate qualification for statesmanship. The debâcle of the Boxer Rebellion forced Empress Dowager Cixi to initiate a number of reforms. These included abolishing the imperial examinations in 1905.

Recommended Reading

Nagel's *Encyclopedia-Guide to China* has a wealth of historical information about Beijing. A number of attractive coffee-table books published about the capital include the Time-Life volume *Peking*, written by David Bonavia, with excellent photographs by Peter Griffiths, and Leong Ka Tai's photographic essay, *Beijing* (Times Edition Singapore), with a text by Frank Ching.

There are some books written by foreigners who have lived in Beijing in recent years which offer particular insight into Chinese life and politics. Bernard Frolic's *Mao's People* (Harvard), Simon Ley's *Broken Images* (Allison & Busby) and *Chinese Shadows* (Viking) and David Bonavia's *The Chinese* (Penguin) are highly informative and readable. Ruth Sidel gives a detailed description of the structure of life in a Beijing neighbourhood in her *Families of Fengsheng — Urban Life in China* (Penguin), while Beverley Hooper tells of student life in *Inside Peking* (MacDonald & Jane's). One of the first western journalists to be accredited in the aftermath of the Cultural Revolution, the correspondent of *Der Spiegel* Tizano Terzani, published his experiences in *The Forbidden Door* (Asia 2000 Ltd) after he was expelled from China in 1984.

The end of the Qing Dynasty is graphically portrayed in two autobiographies — *Two Years in the Forbidden City* by De Ling, a Manchu princess who was lady-in-waiting to the Empress Dowager Cixi, and *From Emperor to Citizen* (Beijing Foreign Languages Press) by the last emperor, Puyi. Marina Warner's biography of the Empress Dowager, *The Dragon Empress* (Weidenfeld & Nicolson), is particularly entertaining. The old Qing Summer Palace, Yuanmingyuan, is described in great detail, accompanied by reproductions of contemporary paintings and copperplate etchings, in *Yuanmingyuan* (Joint Publishing), currently available only with a Chinese text.

Those interested in reading some of China's classical novels will enjoy *Dream of the Red Chamber* by the 18th-century novelist Cao Xueqin — translated as *The Story of the Stone* by David Hawkes and John Minford (5 volumes, Penguin), or as *A Dream of Red Mansions* (3 volumes, Beijing Foreign Languages Press), rendered into English by Yang Hsien-yi and Gladys Yang. A garden featured in the novel — Daguanyuan — is being recreated as a park in the southwest of Beijing.

Life in pre-revolutionary China is vividly portrayed in *Rickshaw: The Novel of Luotuo Xiangzi* by Lao She (University Press of Hawaii), and *Family* by Ba Jin (Doubleday) — both well worth reading. *The Selected Stories of Lu Xun*, China's best-loved 20th-century writer, is translated by Yang Hsien-yi and Gladys Yang for Beijing Foreign Languages Press.

A contemporary poet and writer of fiction who has been hailed as a new voice in the post-Cultural Revolution literary scene is Beijing-born Zhao

Zhenkai (pen-name Bei Dao), whose collection of short stories, *Waves*, has been translated by Bonnie S. McDougall and Susette Ternent Cooke (The Chinese University Press, Hong Kong). *Seeds of Fire: Chinese Voices of Conscience*, edited by Geremie Barmé and John Minford, is an anthology of writings — poetry, essays and extracts from novels — representing the new 'literature of conscience'. It is published by Far Eastern Economic Review and distributed by China Guides Series in Hong Kong.

For a good picture of life in the foreign community in Beijing in the 1920s read Ann Bridge's novel *Peking Picnic* (Triad Granada). Recent reprints by Oxford University Press in their 'Oxford in Asia' paperback series provide interesting background reading on Beijing in the '30s — Osbert Sitwell's *Escape with Me!* and Harold Acton's *Peonies and Ponies*. In the same series are Peter Fleming's *The Siege at Peking* and *Peking* by Juliet Bredon. Oxford University Press's *A Photographer in Old Peking* is a beautiful volume of rare black-and-white photographs taken between 1933 and 1946, interspersed with an evocative account of people and places by the photographer Hedda Morrison.

Hong Kong University Press has published a comprehensive book on *The Ming Tombs*, written by Anne Paludan.

For those with a special interest in the subject, Elizabeth Halston's *Peking Opera* (Oxford University Press) is one of the best books in English. A concise paperback on the subject appeared in 1981 in Beijing — *Peking Opera and Mei Lanfang: a Guide to China's Traditional Theatre and the Arts of its Great Master* by Wu Zuguang, Huang Zuolin and Mei Shaowu (New World Press). *Mei Lanfang — Leader of the Pear Garden* by A.C. Scott is written with much absorbing background (Hong Kong University Press).

A Guide to Pronouncing Chinese Names

The official system of romanization used in China, which the visitor will find on maps, road signs and city shopfronts, is known as *Pinyin*. It is now almost universally adopted by the western media.

Non-Chinese may initially encounter some difficulty in pronouncing romanized Chinese words. In fact many of the sounds correspond to the usual pronunciation of the letters in English. The exceptions are:

Initials

c	is like the *ts* in 'i*ts*'
q	is like the *ch* in '*ch*eese'
x	has no English equivalent, and can best be described as a hissing consonant that lies somewhere between *sh* and *s*. The sound was rendered as *hs* under an earlier transcription system.
z	is like the *ds* in 'fa*ds*'
zh	is unaspirated, and sounds like the *j* in '*j*ug'

Finals

a	sounds like 'ah'
e	is pronounced as in 'h*e*r'
i	is pronounced as in 'sk*i*' (written as *yi* when not preceded by an initial consonant). However, in *ci*, *chi*, *ri*, *shi*, *zi* and *zhi*, the sound represented by the *i* final is quite different and is similar to the *ir* in 's*ir*', but without much stressing of the *r* syllable.
o	sounds like the *aw* in 'l*aw*'
u	sounds like the *oo* in '*oo*ze'
ü	is pronounced as the German *ü* (written as *yu* when not preceded by an initial consonant)

Finals in Combination

When two or more finals are combined, such as in *hao*, *jiao* and *liu*, each letter retains its sound value as indicated in the list above, but note the following:

ai	is like the *ie* in 't*ie*'
ei	is like the *ay* in 'b*ay*'
ian	is like the *ien* in 'Vi*en*na'
ie	similar to 'ear'
ou	is like the *o* in 'c*o*de
uai	sounds like 'why'
uan	is like the *uan* in 'ig*uan*a' (except when preceded by *j*, *q*, *x* and *y*; in these cases a *u* following any of these four consonants is in fact *ü* and *uan* is similar to *uen*.)
ue	is like the *ue* in 'd*ue*t'
ui	sounds like 'way'

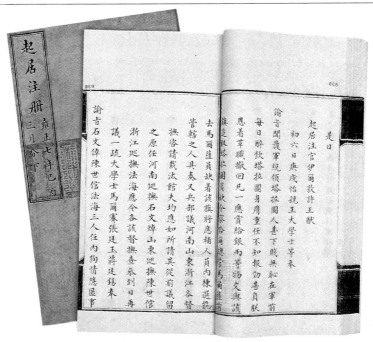

Administrative records from the reign of
Emperor Yongzheng, Palace Museum collection

Examples

A few Chinese names are shown below with English phonetic spelling beside them:

Beijing	Bay-jing
Cixi	Tsi-shi
Guilin	Gway-lin
Hangzhou	Hahng-jo
Kangxi	Kahn-shi
Qianlong	Chien-lawng
Tiantai	Tien-tie
Xi'an	Shi-ahn

An apostrophe is used to separate syllables in certain compound-character words to preclude confusion. For example, *Changan* (which can be *chang-an* or *chan-gan*) is sometimes written as *Chang'an*.

Tones

A Chinese syllable consists of not only an initial and a final or finals, but also a tone or pitch of the voice when the words are spoken. In *Pinyin* the four basic tones are marked ˉ, ´, ˇ and `. These marks are almost never shown in printed form except in language texts.

Chronology of Periods in Chinese History

Palaeolithic	c.600,000–7000 BC
Neolithic	c.7000–1600 BC
Shang	c.1600–1027 BC
Western Zhou	1027–771 BC
Eastern Zhou	770–256 BC
Spring and Autumn Annals	770–476 BC
Warring States	475–221 BC
Qin	221–207 BC
Western (Former) Han	206 BC–8 AD
Xin	9–24
Eastern (Later) Han	25–220
Three Kingdoms	220–265
Western Jin	265–316
Northern and Southern Dynasties	317–589
Sixteen Kingdoms	317–439
□ Former Zhao	304–329
□ Former Qin	351–383
□ Later Qin	384–417
Northern Wei	386–534
Western Wei	535–556
Northern Zhou	557–581
Sui	581–618
Tang	618–907
Five Dynasties	907–960
Northern Song	960–1127
Southern Song	1127–1279
Jin (Jurchen)	1115–1234
Yuan (Mongol)	1279–1368
Ming	1368–1644
Qing (Manchu)	1644–1911
Republic	1911–1949
People's Republic	1949–

Useful Addresses

Embassies

Albania
28 Guanghua Lu, Jianguomenwai tel. 511120
亚尔巴尼亚　建国门外光华路28号

Argentina
11 Sanlitun Dongwu Jie tel. 522090
阿根廷　三里屯东五街11号

Australia
15 Dongzhimenwai Dajie, Sanlitun
tel. 522331
澳大利亚　三里屯东直门外大街15号

Austria
5 Xiushui Nan Jie, Jianguomenwai
tel. 522063
奥地利　建国门外秀水南街5号

Bangladesh
42 Guanghua Lu, Jianguomenwai tel. 522521
孟加拉国　建国门外光华路28号

Belgium
6 Sanlitun Lu tel. 521736
比利时　三里屯6号

Brazil
27 Guanghua Lu, Jianguomenwai tel. 522698
巴西　建国门外光华路27号

Burma
6 Dongzhimenwai Dajie, Sanlitun tel. 521425
缅甸　三里屯东直门外大街6号

Canada
10 Sanlitun Lu tel. 521475
加拿大　三里屯10号

Czechoslovakia
Ritan Lu, Jianguomenwai tel. 521530
捷克斯拉夫　建国门外日坛路

Denmark
1 Sanlitun Dongwu Jie tel. 522431
丹麦　三里屯东五街1号

Finland
30 Guanghua Lu, Jianguomenwai tel. 521753
芬兰　建国门外光华路30号

France
3 Sanlitun Dongsan Jie tel. 521331
法国　三里屯东三街3号

German Democratic Republic
3 Sanlitun Dongsi Jie tel. 521631
东德国　三里屯东四街3号

Germany, Federal Republic of
5 Dongzhimenwai Dajie, Sanlitun
tel. 522161
西德国　三里屯东直门外大街5号

Ghana
8 Sanlitun Lu tel. 521319
加纳　三里屯8号

India
1 Ritan Dong Lu, Jianguomenwai tel. 521908
印度　建国门外日坛东路1号

Italy
2 Sanlitun Donger Jie tel. 522131
意大利　三里屯东二街2号

Japan
7 Ritan Lu, Jianguomenwai tel. 522361
日本　建国门外日坛路7号

Jordan
54 Sanlitun Dongliu Jie tel. 523906
约旦　三里屯东六街54号

Kampuchea
9 Dongzhimenwai Dajie tel. 521889
柬埔寨　东直门外大街

Kenya
4 Sanlitun Xiliu Jie tel. 523381
肯尼亚　三里屯西六街

Kuwait
23 Guanghua Lu, Jianguomenwai tel. 522182
科威特　建国门外光华路23号

Laos
11 Sanlitun Dongsi Jie tel. 521224
老挝　三里屯东四街11号

Malaysia
13 Dongzhimenwai Dajie, Sanlitun
tel. 522531
马来西亚　三里屯东直门外大街13号

Nepal
1 Sanlitun Xiliu Jie tel. 521795
尼泊尔　三里屯西六街1号

Netherlands
10 Sanlitun Dongsi Jie tel. 521131
荷兰　三里屯东四街10号

New Zealand
1 Donger Jie Ritan, Jianguomenwai
tel. 522731
新西兰　建国门外日坛东二街1号

Nigeria
2 Dongwu Jie, Sanlitun Bei tel. 523631
尼日利亚　三里屯东五街2号

Norway
1 Sanlitun Dongyi Jie tel. 522261
挪威　三里屯东一街1号

Pakistan
1 Dongzhimenwai Dajie, Sanlitun
tel. 522504
巴基斯坦　三里屯东直门外大街1号

Philippines
23 Xiushui Bei Jie, Jianguomenwai
tel. 522794
菲律宾　建国门外秀水北街23号

Poland
1 Ritan Lu, Jianguomenwai tel. 521235
波兰　建国门外日坛路1号

Sierra Leone
7 Dongzhimenwai Dajie, Sanlitun
tel. 521446
塞拉利昂　三里屯东直门外大街7号

Singapore
4 Liangmahe Nan Lu, Sanlitun tel. 523926
新加坡　三里屯亮马河南路4号

Spain
9 Sanlitun Lu tel. 523629
西班牙　三里屯路9号

Sri Lanka
3 Jianhua Lu, Jianguomenwai tel. 521906
斯里兰卡　建国门外建华路3号

Sweden
3 Dongzhimenwai Dajie, Sanlitun
tel. 523331
瑞典　三里屯东直门外大街3号

Switzerland
3 Sanlitun Dongwu Jie tel. 522736
瑞士　三里屯东五街3号

Tanzania
53 Sanlitun, Dongliu Jie tel. 521408
坦桑尼亚　三里屯东六街53号

Thailand
40 Guanghua Lu, Jianguomenwai tel. 521903
泰国　建国门外光华路40号

Uganda
5 Sanlitun Dong Jie tel. 521708
乌干达　三里屯东街5号

United Kingdom
11 Guanghua Lu, Jianguomenwai tel. 521961
英国　建国门外光华路11号

USA
(Consular section)
2 Xiushui Dong Jie, Jianguomenwai
tel. 523831
美国　建国门外秀水东街2号

USSR
4 Dongzhimen Beizhong Jie tel. 522051
苏联　东直门北中街4号

Venezuela
14 Sanlitun Lu tel. 521295
委内瑞拉　三里屯路14号

Vietnam
32 Guanghua Lu, Jianguomenwai tel. 521155
越南　建国门外光华路32号

Yugoslavia
56 Sanlitun Dongliu Jie tel. 521562
南斯拉夫　三里屯东六街56号

Zambia
5 Sanlitun Dongsi Jie tel. 521554
赞比亚　三里屯东四街5号

Airlines

Aeroflot Soviet Airlines
5−53 Jianguomenwai tel. 523581
苏联航空公司　建国门外5-53号

Air France
12−72 Jianguomenwai tel. 523894
法国航空公司　建国门外12-72号

Alitalia
150 Jianguomenwai tel. 5002233
意大利航空公司　建国门外150号

British Airways
12−61 Jianguomenwai tel. 523601
(Reservations)
英国航空公司　建国门外12-61号

CAAC Main Office
117 Dongsi Xi Dajie tel. 553275
中国民航总局　东四西大街117号

CAAC (Beijing Hotel)
Chang'an Dajie tel. 5007317
中国民航(北京饭店)　长安大街

CAAC (Great Wall Sheraton)
Donghuan Bei Lu tel. 5002272
中国民航(长城饭店)　东环北路

Cathay Pacific Airways
Room 152, Jianguo Hotel, Jianguomenwai
tel. 5003339
国泰航空公司　建国门外建国饭店152房

Ethiopian Airlines
12−32 Jianguomenwai tel. 523812
埃塞俄比亚航空公司　建国门外12-32号

Iran Air
12−63 Jianguomenwai tel. 523843
伊朗航空公司　建国门外12-63号

Japan Airlines
Jinglun Hotel, Jianguomenwai. tel. 5002221
日本航空公司　建国门外京伦饭店

JAT Yugoslav Airlines
2−2−162 Jianguomenwai tel. 523486
南斯拉夫航空公司　建国门外2-2-162号

Chosonminhang
Ritan Bei Lu, Jianguomenwai tel. 523981
朝鲜民用航空局　建国门外日坛北路

Lufthansa
Great Wall Sheraton, Donghuan Bei Lu
tel. 5001616
德国航空公司　东环北路长城饭店

Northwest Orient
Jianguo Hotel, Jianguomenwai tel. 502233
ext. 140
西北航空公司　建国门外建国饭店

Pakistan International Airlines
12−43 Jianguomenwai tel. 523274
巴基斯坦国际航空公司　建国门外12-43号

Philippine Airlines
12−53 Jianguomenwai tel. 523992
菲律宾航空公司　建国门外12-53号

Qantas Airways
Jinglun Hotel, Jianguomenwai tel. 502481
澳大利亚航空公司　建国门外京伦饭店

Singapore Airlines
1−2 CITIC Building, Jianguomenwai
tel. 504138
新加坡航空公司　建国门外国际大厦1-2号

Swissair
5th Floor, 12−33 Jianguomenwai tel. 52328
瑞士航空公司　建国门外12-33号六楼

Tarom Romanian Air Transport
Ritan Donger Lu, Jianguomenwai tel. 52355
罗马尼亚空运公司　建国门外日坛东二路

Thai International
Room 343, Arcade, Great Wall Sheraton,
Donghuan Bei Lu tel. 5005566 ext. 2271
泰国国际航空公司
东环北路长城饭店343号店

United Airlines
Rooms 135–137, Jinglun Hotel,
Jianguomenwai tel. 5001985
联合航空公司　建国门外京伦饭店135-137房

United China Airlines
West Building, Beijing Hotel, Chang'an
Dajie tel. 507766, 507598
中国联合航空公司　长安大街北京饭店西座

Airport

Beijing International Airport
Switchboard (Chinese-speaking) tel. 558341
Switchboard (Foreigners) tel. 552931,
523231
Inquiries (all airlines) tel. 552515
北京国际机场

Taxis

Beijing Car Co.
Maquan, Guangqumenwai tel. 594441
Bus (telephone order) 552287
Taxi (telephone order) 557661
北京出租汽车公司　广渠门外马泉

Capital Car Co.
10 Yuetan Bei Jie, Xichengqu tel. 867084,
863661
(English-speaking dispatch) tel. 557461
首都出租汽车公司　西城区月坛北街10号

Railways

Main Railway Station
Tel. (Inquiries) 554866, 5576851, 5582042
Baggage
Tel. (Domestic and international arrivals)
5582372, 556956, 556028
Customs
Tel. (Export) 551619, (Import) 556242,
(Foreigners' office) 5582042
北京火车站

Xizhimen Railway Station
Xizhimenwai tel. 8996223
西直门火车站

Bicycle Rental

Dongdan Bicycle Repair Service
Dongdan Bei Dajie tel. 552752
东单自行车修理店　东单北大街

Limin Bicycle Shop
2 Chongwenmenwai Dajie
利民自行车修理站　崇文门外大街2号

Jianguomenwai Bicycle Shop
Jianguomenwai Dajie (opposite Friendship
Store) tel. 592391
建国门外自行车商店　建国门外大街

Xidan Bicycle Repair Workshop
Xuanwumennei Dajie tel. 332472
西单自行车修理部　宣武门内大街

Travel Agencies

American Express International Inc.
Jinglun Hotel tel. 5002266, tx. 210172
美国运通国际股份有限公司　京伦饭店

Beijing Tradewinds
Room 114, 1st Floor, International Club,
Jianguomenwai tel. 595927, 595997,
tx. 210304
北京国际四季风服务有限公司
建国门外国际俱乐部二楼114室

**CITS (China International Travel
Service), Beijing Branch Main Office**
Chongwenmen Hotel, 2 Qianmen Dong
Dajie tel. 755017, tx. 20052
中国国际旅行社北京分社
前门东大街2号崇文门饭店

CITS, Beijing Branch
Jinglun Hotel, Jianguomenwai tel. 5002266
ext. 2041
中国国际旅行社北京分社
建国门外京伦饭店

CITS, Beijing Branch
Huadu Hotel, 8 Xinyuan Nan Lu tel. 5001166
ext. 2204
中国国际旅行社北京分社
新源南路8号华都饭店

CITS, Beijing Branch
Great Wall Sheraton, Donghuan Bei Lu,
tel. 5005566 ext. 2269
中国国际旅行社北京分社
东环北路长城饭店

CITS Head Office
6 Dong Chang'an Jie tel. 5121122, tx. 22350
中国国际旅行社总社　东长安街6号

**CTS (China Travel Service), Beijing
Branch**
2 Qianmen Dong Dajie tel. 755448, tx. 22489
中国旅行社北京分社　前门东大街2号

CTS, Head Office
8 Dongjiaomin Xiang tel. 553491, tx. 22487
中国旅行社总办事处　东交民巷8号

CYTS (China Youth Travel Service)
23 Dongjiaomin Xiang tel. 551531, tx. 20024
中国青年旅行社　东交民巷23号

Intourist
1 USSR Embassy, 4 Dongzhimen Beizhong
Jie tel. 521267
苏联国际旅行社　东直门北中街1号

Banking Representative Offices

Bank of America
West Building, 23 Qianmen Dong Dajie
tel. 552685, tx. 22562
美国美洲银行　前门东大街23号西座

Bank of China (Beijing Branch)
32 Dengshikou Xi Jie tel. 557531, tx. 22491
中国银行北京分行　灯市口西街32号

Bank of Tokyo
Room 2088, Beijing Hotel tel. 507766
ext. 2088, tx. 22420
东京银行　北京饭店2088房

Barclays Bank
West Building, 23 Qianmen Dong Dajie
tel. 552417, tx. 22589
英国巴克莱银行　前门东大街23号西座

**The Hongkong and Shanghai Banking
Corporation**
Room 149, Jianguo Hotel tel. 592294,
tx. 22429
香港上海汇丰银行　建国饭店149房

The Royal Bank of Canada
Room 5088, Beijing Hotel tel. 507766
ext. 5088, tx. 22586
加拿大皇家银行　北京饭店5088房

Standard Chartered Bank
Rooms 117-9, Jianguo Hotel tel. 5002233
ext. 119, tx. 20439
标准渣打（麦加利）银行　建国饭店117-9房

Theatres and Cinemas

Beijing Concert Hall
Bei Xinhua Jie tel. 657006
北京音乐厅　北新华街

Beijing Drama Theatre
11 Hufang Lu, Xuanwuqu tel. 338149,
330537
北京戏剧院　宣武区虎坊路11号

Beijing Opera Theatre
Hufangqiao tel. 335390
北京京剧院　虎坊桥

Capital Cinema
46 Xi Chang'an Jie tel. 656575
首都电影院　西长安街46号

Capital Theatre
22 Wangfujing Dajie tel. 550978, 557213
首都剧场　王府井大街22号

Central Music Conservatory Auditorium
Xi Wenhua Jie Xikou, Xidan Nan tel. 665382
中央音乐学院礼堂　西单南西文化街西口

Chinese Opera Theatre
34 Baishiqiao Lu, Haidianqu tel. 894703,
895144, 894612
中国京剧院　海淀区白石桥路34号

China Opera and Dance Theatre
2 Nanhua Dong Jie, Hufang Lu tel. 330252
中国歌剧舞剧院　虎坊路南华东街2号

International Club Theatre
International Club, Ritan Lu, Jianguomenwai
tel. 592207
国际俱乐部剧场　建国门外日坛路国际俱乐部

Nationalities Cultural Palace Auditorium
Fuxingmennei Dajie tel. 662530
民族文化宫礼堂　复兴门内大街

Sports Facilities

Beijing Gymnasium
4 Tiyuguan Lu, Chongwenmenwai
tel. 757381 ext. 502
北京体育馆　崇文门外体育馆路4号

Beijing Workers' Gymnasium
Gongren Tiyuchang Bei Lu tel. 592961
北京工人体育馆　工人体育场北路

Beijing Workers' Stadium
Gongren Tiyuchang Bei Lu tel. 592961
北京工人体育场　工人体育场北路

Shoudu Gymnasium
Baishiqiao tel. 890281
首都体育馆　白石桥

Post and Telecommunications

Beijing Main PTT (Post, Telephone and Telecommunications) Bureau
Dianbao Dalou, Fuxingmennei Dajie
tel. 664900, 664426, 666296
北京总邮电局　复兴门内大街电报大楼

Beijing Hotel PTT (Express mail service)
Beijing Hotel, lobby concourse tel. 555358
北京饭店邮电业务特快专达组
北京饭店门廊

Beijing Telecommunications Bureau
131 Xidan Dajie tel. 667700, 661435
北京电信局　西单大街131号

DHL China Office
Xiao Liangmaqiao, Liangmaqiao Lu
tel. 481643
中国对外贸易运输公司　小亮马桥亮马桥路

Dongdan Post Office (Parcel service)
23 Dongdan Bei Dajie. tel. 555043, 555265
东单邮局包裹处　东单北大街

International Post Office (Parcel service)
121 Yongan Lu, Tianqiao tel. 337853,
337717
国际邮局　天桥永安路121号

International Posts and Telecommunications Service (Express mail service)
23 Dongdan Bei Dajie. tel. 336621
国际邮电信业务特快专达组
东单北大街23号

Sanlitun PTT
1-3-11 Sanlitun Bei tel. 521085
三里屯邮电信业务　三里屯1-3-11

Miscellaneous

Beijing Municipal Public Security Bureau (Foreigners section)
85 Beichizi Jie tel. 553102
北京公安局外事科　北池子街85号

Beijing University
Yiheyuan Lu, Haidianqu tel. 282471
北京大学　海淀区颐和园路

China International Exhibition Centre
6 Beisanhuan Xi Lu, Chaoyang tel. 481798,
481745, tx. 210214
中国国际展览馆　朝阳北三环西路6号

Capital Hospital
1 Shuaifuyuan Hutong, Wangfujing
tel. 553731
首都医院　王府井师府园胡同1号

Erligou Negotiations Building
Xizhimenwai Dajie tel. 890931
二里沟谈判楼　西直门外大街

International Club
Jianguomenwai tel. 522254
国际俱乐部　建国门外

Index of Places